CHRISTIAN HEROES: THEN & NOW

PAUL BRAND

Helping Hands

CHRISTIAN HEROES: THEN & NOW

PAUL BRAND

Helping Hands

JANET & GEOFF BENGE

YWAM
PUBLISHING
P.O. BOX 55787   SEATTLE, WA 98155

YWAM Publishing is the publishing ministry of Youth With A Mission. Youth With A Mission (YWAM) is an international missionary organization of Christians from many denominations dedicated to presenting Jesus Christ to this generation. To this end, YWAM has focused its efforts in three main areas: (1) training and equipping believers for their part in fulfilling the Great Commission (Matthew 28:19), (2) personal evangelism, and (3) mercy ministry (medical and relief work).

For a free catalog of books and materials, call (425) 771-1153 or (800) 922-2143. Visit us online at www.ywampublishing.com.

Paul Brand: Helping Hands
Copyright © 2011 by YWAM Publishing

Published by YWAM Publishing
a ministry of Youth With A Mission
P.O. Box 55787, Seattle, WA 98155

First printing 2011

ISBN 978-1-57658-536-8

Library of Congress Cataloging-in-Publication Data is on file with the publisher and the Library of Congress.

Unless otherwise noted, Scripture quotations are taken from the New King James Version, Copyright © 1979, 1980, 1982 by Thomas Nelson, Inc., Publishers. Used by permission.

Printed in the United States of America.

CHRISTIAN HEROES: THEN & NOW

Adoniram Judson

Amy Carmichael

Betty Greene

Brother Andrew

Cameron Townsend

Clarence Jones

Corrie ten Boom

Count Zinzendorf

C. S. Lewis

C. T. Studd

David Bussau

David Livingstone

D. L. Moody

Elisabeth Elliot

Eric Liddell

Florence Young

George Müller

Gladys Aylward

Hudson Taylor

Ida Scudder

Isobel Kuhn

Jacob DeShazer

Jim Elliot

John Wesley

John Williams

Jonathan Goforth

Lillian Trasher

Loren Cunningham

Lottie Moon

Mary Slessor

Nate Saint

Paul Brand

Rachel Saint

Rowland Bingham

Sundar Singh

Wilfred Grenfell

William Booth

William Carey

*Unit study curriculum guides
are available for select biographies.*

*Available at your local Christian
bookstore or from YWAM Publishing
1-800-922-2143 / www.ywampublishing.com*

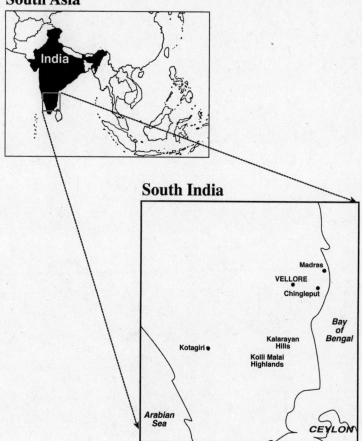

South Asia

India

South India

Madras
VELLORE
Chingleput

Bay
of
Bengal

Kalarayan
Hills
Kotagiri
Kolli Malai
Highlands

Arabian
Sea

CEYLON

Contents

Contents

Chapter 1

On the Road to Chingleput

Paul Brand walked along the side of the dark road, his two helpers beside him, boxes of specimen jars and instruments hoisted onto their shoulders. The trio had walked two miles from their fire-ravaged vehicle, hoping that someone would come along and pick them up. As they trudged on, their hope faded. Not a single car or bus had passed them. Only bullock carts were heading in the opposite direction, passing like shadows in the night. Paul kept a weary eye to the east, wondering whether they would still be walking when dawn broke. By then it would be too late.

Paul's mood brightened when he realized that the next town was home to a Christian mission school. Perhaps they would find someone at the school who could drive them the rest of the way to Chingleput.

When they reached the school a short time later, Paul roused the teacher from his bed.

"I'm sorry. I don't have a car, but I can offer you all a bed for the remainder of the night," the bleary-eyed teacher responded.

"No, no, you don't understand. We have to get to Chingleput as soon as possible. We haven't come this far to give up now."

Paul persuaded the teacher to get dressed and go in search of a car and driver they could hire. Even Paul knew this was a tall order. It was after midnight. To Paul's relief, the teacher returned with a driver willing to take the team to their destination.

Soon Paul and his assistants were bumping their way along the potholed road toward Chingleput. At two-thirty in the morning, weary from the journey, they pulled up to the gate of the leprosarium. Everything was dark and quiet. Paul banged on the gate, and an old watchman carrying a kerosene hurricane lamp shuffled over to see what the commotion was.

"I'm Dr. Paul Brand," Paul announced. "Dr. Harry Paul has given me and my team permission to enter the grounds to perform an autopsy. Please take us to the body."

The night watchman recoiled at Paul's words and signaled with his hands that he wanted nothing to do with the conversation. Paul took a deep breath and told the watchman that he was not about to turn around and leave, especially after all he had been through to get this far. Eventually the night watchman relented and told the group to follow him. Once again the team hoisted the instruments and specimen jars onto their shoulders and followed the old man as he led them behind some huts and then upward along a winding, rocky trail.

They walked at a brisk pace, and Paul marveled at the situation. As a boy growing up in South India, he could never have imagined this scene. The one thing he had determined he would never be when he grew up was a medical doctor. And like everyone else, he had been taught to fear leprosy. But now here he was, a doctor on his way to one of the most exciting events of his life, performing an autopsy on the body of a leprosy patient. His life had certainly taken some dramatic turns from those carefree days growing up in the Kolli Malai highlands.

Chapter 2

The Strange Visitors

Seven-year-old Paul Brand sat on a branch midway up a jackfruit tree. No matter how many times he climbed the tree, he always loved to stop and peer out over the clumps of bamboo at the rolling hills beyond. The hills stretched as far as he could see. Closer to home were the fields where his father showed the hill people how to plant orange trees and sugar cane.

As Paul surveyed the countryside from his perch in the tree, a movement caught his eye. Someone—or maybe a group of people—was walking very slowly up the track toward the house. Paul squinted into the sun. There was always a constant procession of visitors who came to the Brands' simple home high in the hill country of southeastern India.

15

Paul knew that his parents, Jesse and Evelyn Brand, were well loved by the local people of the Kolli Hills. Paul had lived in the highlands his entire life and had seen thousands of people seek out his parents for all kinds of help and advice. Sometimes people wanted his father to help them with a building or to check on the composition of the bricks he had taught them to make. Other times they wanted Paul's mother to demonstrate one more time how to tuck a baby under a mosquito net at night to greatly increase the child's chance of survival, or to explain why it was necessary to go to all the trouble of walling off a village's water well.

Paul knew that this was not the only reason his parents had left their native England to come to the hill country of India. Every night before bed his parents prayed for their neighbors, asking God to help them understand that there was one swami, or religious person, whom they needed to know—Swami Jesus. As far as Paul could tell, his parents' nightly prayers had little effect. No one other than a shepherd boy had ever taken an interest in becoming a follower of Jesus.

As Paul sat in the tree, his attention was diverted when he spotted his four-year-old sister, Connie, below him. Paul was tempted to drop a jackfruit "bomb" near her, but then he remembered how his mother hated it when they got the sticky sap from the jackfruit on their clothes or skin.

"Hey, Connie," Paul called to his sister as he shimmied down the tree trunk. "Do you want to go looking for frogs?"

Connie nodded, her golden blonde curls blowing in the wind. Together the two children wandered over to a woodpile where they had heard croaking noises the past few nights.

No sooner had Paul and Connie started poking around the rocks by the woodpile with sticks than three men, the group Paul had seen from up in the jackfruit tree, shuffled into sight. Paul stared at them. There was something unsettlingly different about these visitors, and Paul strained to figure out what it was. All three men were dressed like many other poor Indian men: a dusty blanket draped over the shoulder, a faded turban, and a breechcloth. But as he scanned their feet, Paul became alarmed. The men had stubby, bleeding feet, and although Paul had been taught not to stare, he was certain that some had missing toes. Then Paul noticed that the men's hands were much the same as their feet. Two of them had swollen hands with open sores. The other hid his hands behind his back.

"Get back, children!" Paul turned to see his mother standing beside them. Her voice was strained and high pitched. "Paul, run and get your father. Take Constance with you. And don't come back. Stay in the house."

Alarmed by the strange urgency in his mother's voice, Paul grabbed Connie by the hand and ran toward the house as he yelled for his father.

Jesse Brand came quickly, and Paul watched him hurry toward the three visitors.

"Come on, Paul. Mummy told us to stay inside," Connie pleaded as she ran up the four steps and into the house.

Paul shook his head. "You stay inside, Connie, and I will find out what's going on and come back and tell you."

Connie frowned as Paul glanced back at his parents. The three men were kneeling around Paul's father. Paul had witnessed hundreds of strangers who came for medical attention do the same thing, and every time, Jesse would reach down and help them to their feet. He would explain that he did not want to be worshiped, that Swami Jesus was the only One worthy of their worship. But this time Paul noticed that his father did not reach down to lift up even one of the men. Instead, Jesse stood with his hands limp at his sides, a sad look on his face.

Paul slipped behind a bush. Slowly, so as not to attract attention, he crawled from one rock or clump of grass to another until he found a good vantage point to see what was going on.

Paul listened to his father and the three men converse in Tamil. Having been born and raised in southeastern India, Paul spoke the language as fluently as he spoke English. Paul's father shook his head. "I'm sorry. There is very little we can do for you, but we will do what we can. You stay here and don't move. I'll be right back."

Jesse dashed back to the house while Paul's mother stood by awkwardly. Although she had been in India for ten years, Evelyn did not speak Tamil well enough to chat with people.

Two minutes later Jesse returned. Much to Paul's relief, he did not seem to have noticed that Connie was in the house alone. Jesse put down a basin of water and then pulled on a pair of gloves. Paul frowned. His father wore gloves only when he was performing an operation, but there were no operating instruments, just bandages and a can of ointment.

Leaning forward a little, Paul watched intently as his father gently bathed each man's feet, smeared them with ointment, and bandaged them. Paul's mother went inside the house and returned with a basket of vegetables and half a cooked chicken. Paul grimaced. He had been looking forward to eating the chicken for dinner. Evelyn set the basket on the ground in front of the three strangers and gestured for one of the men to pick it up. "Basket. You take and keep," she said in halting Tamil. This action was puzzling to Paul, since his mother used the basket every day to store her vegetables.

Paul watched as the last man had his feet wrapped in bandages, and he wondered what would happen next. The Brands often invited strangers to stay the night in the open space under the house before continuing on their way, but not today. One of the men stooped over and wrapped the food from the basket in his blanket. The men thanked Paul's parents and walked back down the path. Jesse carried the basin and ointment inside.

This was all a bit confusing to Paul. There was something very gloomy about the exchange between his parents and the three men. His parents normally talked with their patients and gave them advice, but this time there had been none of that. A few minutes later, Paul wandered over to where the men had crouched.

"No, Paul! Don't touch it!" Evelyn yelled as her son bent down to pick up the basket and return it to her. She came running up behind Paul. "And stay away from the place where the men were. Don't walk on it or play there. Do you understand?" she demanded.

Paul nodded as he watched his father light a match and set the basket on fire.

"Why did you do that?" Paul asked. "Mother needs that basket."

As Jesse turned to reply, Paul could see tears in his father's eyes. "Because, son," he said, "those men were lepers."

Paul felt a chill go down his spine. He knew about lepers from the Bible stories his parents read to him. In the Old Testament Naaman had been a leper, and in the New Testament Jesus had healed lepers. But now Paul had seen three lepers with his own eyes.

Although he never had the courage to bring the subject up again, Paul often thought about the three lepers. He wondered whether anyone else was cleaning their wounds, or if any more of their fingers or toes had fallen off. But as much as he felt sorry for the men, Paul could never in a million years imagine himself looking after strangers the way his parents did. Even though he was only seven, he already thought he had seen too much.

Guinea worms were one thing that repulsed Paul. They were a constant problem in the neighboring villages, and Jesse removed hundreds of them, one inch at a time. Paul had seen it done so many times that he knew the procedure exactly. First his father would find the outline of the guinea worm under the person's skin, and then he would have the person bathe that part of his or her body in cold water. It took only a few minutes for the guinea worm to pierce the skin with its tail and begin laying eggs in the water. That was when Jesse would grab the tail. Paul knew that once you had a grip on the tail, you couldn't just pull the worm straight out. If you did, the worm would break in two and die inside the person's body, causing a serious and often fatal infection. To get rid of a guinea worm, you had to gently pull about two inches of the worm's tail out and wind it around a small stick. Each day after that, the patient would come back and have Paul's father wind another two inches of the worm out until the creature was completely extracted. Sometimes the worm was up to three feet long.

One particular incident affected Paul so much that he could hardly bear to watch his father practice medicine again. Paul and his father were visiting a village when a man with a very swollen leg from a guinea-worm infection approached them. Paul watched as his father helped the man hobble over to a grassy hillside and sit down. Then Jesse pulled out a knife, sterilized it with a match, and cut into the man's infected leg. Pus came spouting out, like the pictures Paul had seen of whales spouting water. The pus kept flowing until Jesse had collected a bucketful of the stuff. The smell of the pus and the sight of it oozing from the man's leg overwhelmed Paul, who felt like throwing up. "Filthy infection! Pus everywhere! How can my father stand this? I will never be a doctor!" Paul said to himself as his father removed the dead guinea worm, the source of the infection.

Over the next two years, the Brands kept busy with their missionary work. People kept coming to the house to seek their help, and Paul's parents traveled to outlying villages to bring medical care and share the gospel.

When a gift of money came in from a church in England, Jesse got to work supervising the building of a new chapel in the village of Vazhavanthi. Back in England before Jesse became a missionary, he had been a builder. Paul marveled at how easily his father could supervise building projects and dispense medicine. The new chapel was completed on Christmas Eve, and Paul accompanied his parents to the opening service the following morning.

One of the things that Paul loved to do most of all was read. Sometimes at night in bed he would read by the glow of an insect light—a jar that contained glowworms and fireflies. When combined, the insects gave off just enough light to read by if he held the jar close to the page.

Paul kept his bug-eating sundew plant next to his bed, and at naptime in the afternoons, he would take a fly and drop it on the plant's green leaves tinged with red. When the fly touched a leaf, the leaf would spring closed, engulfing the fly, and then slowly devour it.

In early 1923, when Paul was nearly nine years old, his mother uttered what sounded to him like the strangest words: "We are going home!"

Paul had no idea what she meant. "But we are home, Mummy," he retorted.

His mother gave him a hug. "I know, Paul," she said. "And this will always be your home, but you have another home in England. Imagine that!" Evelyn sounded overly cheerful, and Paul began to wonder what this other home was like.

Paul had never been "home" to England. In fact, he had seldom seen another European. When his mother explained to him about snow and sleet or cars and ocean liners, Paul could scarcely picture such things. But the thing that worried him most about this new home was the prospect of going to an English school.

Paul's mother had taught him how to read and write, and his father's science lessons involved the natural things around them: dissecting an ant hill to find the queen ant or standing very still, watching a snake claim a frog as its prey. Paul even did his math outside. Because he found it hard to concentrate while sitting in the house, his mother allowed him to do his math assignments while sitting high in a tree. Evelyn sat underneath the tree teaching Connie. When Paul had finished a set of math sums, he would tie his book to a rope and lower it down for his mother to check his work. If he got the answers all correct, his mother would tie the book back onto the rope, and Paul would hoist the book back up and do more. If he got some wrong, he had to climb down from the tree so his mother could help him correct his mistakes. Either way, Paul enjoyed his tree school much more than he could ever imagine enjoying a desk in a long row of desks, all occupied by boys in identical uniforms.

As much as he dreaded the idea, however, the day came when it was time for the Brand family to leave the hill country and start the long trip to England. Paul knew that his parents had met briefly in England and had then come to India separately as missionaries, where they met again and eventually married. He also knew that it had been twelve years since his mother and thirteen years since his father had been in England. As Jesse packed up the journals and books he was taking with him, Paul searched his father's face to see whether his father looked any more excited about going to England than he did. Paul did not think so.

Things got even bleaker when Paul's mother explained that they would stop at Madras on the way, where they would buy Paul a pair of lace-up shoes which he would be expected to wear from then on. Paul looked down at his wide, tanned feet, gloomy at the thought of encasing them in tightly strapped shoes. He had a feeling that wearing shoes was not going to be the worst of it.

Chapter 3

Everything Was Gray

The trip to England was an exciting experience for Paul. Most of all, he loved having his father around twenty-four hours a day. Together the two of them explored every inch of the passenger ship they were traveling on. Since he had never been on a ship, Paul was amazed by everything he saw on board, from the huge galley, buzzing with chefs and kitchen hands all working together to prepare meals for the dining room, to the heat and noise of the engine room, where large generators produced power for the vessel and steam turbines turned the propellers. Corridors were everywhere, leading to all sorts of interesting nooks and crannies. The things that surprised and delighted Paul the most were the faucets over the sink and bathtub in the small bathroom of their cabin.

Neither Paul nor Connie had ever seen such items. They were fascinated by the way water flowed from the taps with just a simple turn of the handle. Not only that, but the water coming from the taps was so much cleaner than the hand-drawn well water they were used to in India. And they didn't have to worry about the threat of guinea worms from this water.

Despite Paul's expectations when they set sail from India, the month-long trip aboard ship passed quickly. Paul and the rest of the Brand family were gathered on the aft deck when the English coastline came into view. It was unlike anything Paul had ever seen—mostly flat, green land sloping up from the sea, with rolling hills in the distance wrapped in tendrils of mist. When some impressive white cliffs came into sight, Jesse leaned over, tousled Paul's sandy brown hair, and said, "Those are the White Cliffs of Dover. We're nearly home."

As the ship approached the mouth of the river Thames, Paul felt uneasy. He took a deep breath, knowing that in about two hours relatives would be surrounding him. His mother had warned him that the whole Harris family—her side of the family— would want to hug and kiss him. Paul found such behavior odd. Except for his father, mother, and sister, he had never laid eyes on any members of his family. But these relatives all knew him, or thought they did, through the letters his mother sent home, and now they were waiting to barrage him with affection.

Evelyn Brand had seven older sisters, and Paul listened as Connie recited their names: Aunt Grace,

Aunt Minnie, Aunt Lily, Aunt Rosa, Aunt Eunice, Aunt Florence, and Aunt Hope. Connie then recited the names of the younger Harris siblings: Uncle Charlie, Evelyn, Aunt Stella, and Uncle Bertie.

Paul nodded. His little sister had all the relatives' names down pat, even though she had never met or seen any of them before. As Paul thought about his relatives, he couldn't imagine what it must be like to grow up with ten brothers and sisters.

Connie went on in a singsong voice listing off more information about her mother's brothers and sisters. "Aunt Rosa married Uncle Dick and then had some children and then she died. So Aunt Stella married him and had some more children. And Aunt Grace and Aunt Minnie and Aunt Lily got married, and Aunt Florence married a man from Australia and moved there. Uncle Bertie and Uncle Charlie got married too. That leaves Aunt Eunice and Aunt Hope at home with Grandma, and, of course, Mama off in India."

"Please don't get started on the cousins!" Paul begged, remembering that his mother had told him he had over fifty cousins on her side of the family alone. He'd heard enough about relatives he had never met.

The sight of two tugboats approaching the ship diverted Connie's attention. The boats were moving up the river Thames and approaching the Tilbury docks. Paul watched as the tugs pulled alongside the ship, tied up to the hull, and began moving the ship toward the dock. It was a tight fit, and Paul marveled at how agile the two tugboats were.

The tugs maneuvered the ship alongside the dock at Tilbury, and thick hawsers (ropes) fore and aft were lowered from ship to dock. The looped ends of the hawsers were placed over the bollards on the dock, and the rope flicked taut as the ship was reeled in and snuggly tied up. The ship was secured, and a gangway was hoisted into place. The journey to England was over, and Paul knew it was time to go ashore and meet his relatives.

At the end of the gangway the Brand family were engulfed in the outstretched arms of relatives. Paul and Connie stayed close together, hoping the ordeal would soon be over. And it was. The excitement, the hugs, and the kisses died down, and it was time to climb aboard the train for the trip to Paul's mother's childhood home in St. John's Wood, an upscale suburb in north London.

As the train pulled away from the station, Paul took in the sights. Unlike in India, everyone on this train had a seat. People weren't standing or squatting in the aisle, and no one was riding on top of the train or clinging to its side. Paul stared out the window as the train rolled past streets dotted with houses and people, multistory buildings, lampposts, and cars and buses. The thing he marveled at most was the fact that almost everyone he saw both outside and inside the train was white-skinned. Those outside all seemed to be moving in an orderly manner, stopping at street corners. The men were tipping their hats to each other. It was all so different from the chaotic, colorful streets Paul had witnessed in Madras and Bombay.

After the train ride into London, the Brands made their way to Number 3 Cavendish Street. The house Paul encountered there was unlike anything he could have imagined. He counted three stories of windows in the gray stone walls, and he knew from his mother that the place had a basement. Despite its height, the house, sandwiched between two other villa houses, looked impossibly narrow. It was very different from the home he had left behind in India, with its vantage point on the hill and rolling slopes.

Paul smiled as he entered the house. The inside smelled foreign to him—a mixture of lemon and sweet aromas. His mother took his hand and guided him toward the stairs. "Come with us, Connie," she said. "It's time to meet your grandmother."

Paul shrank back. The thought of meeting his grandmother for the first time confused him. His grandfather had died just months before they left India for England, and Paul was not sure whether to appear happy to meet his grandmother or sad that she had lost her husband.

Paul stood at the door of his grandmother's room on the third floor. A large bed sat to one side, an overstuffed armchair beside it. The rest of the room was cluttered with old mahogany furniture and knickknacks.

Grandmother Harris was over eighty years old and couldn't walk, and she hardly ever left her room. When she was not lying in bed, she would sit in the overstuffed armchair. She especially liked it when her grandchildren visited her. She would sit and tell them all sorts of stories about her ancestors. Paul had to admit that for her age, his grandmother was in amazingly good health. Her cheeks were rosy and not wrinkled in the way many other old women's cheeks were. Her voice was strong and clear, and her eyes seemed to twinkle as she talked and told the children stories and quoted whole chapters of the Bible from memory.

The rest of the first day was a blur. About the only thing that Paul remembered afterward was the delicious dessert that night of jam roly-poly and fresh whipped cream.

The next day the Brand children were allowed to explore the house. They started in the attic, where Paul opened the small window and contemplated tying a rope to the frame and letting himself down to the ground. He decided to leave that activity for another day, and he and Connie continued their exploration. The two of them ended up in the basement breakfast room. The room was dark and gloomy compared to other rooms in the house, but it did not have the same formal feeling that most of those rooms had. The maids Dora and Caroline used the room for folding clothes and other chores. A labyrinth of hallways led to the kitchen, pantry, and cellars. While Paul and Connie were in the basement, Cissie, the family cook, fed them extra tidbits of food, as she called them. Paul immediately knew that this was the place where he and Connie would be spending a lot of time. He could see so many possibilities for games, and he proposed one right away. "How about we see who can go completely around the room without touching the floor once?" he asked Connie.

Connie's eyes lit up with the challenge. Soon brother and sister were climbing from picture rails to dresser tops, sliding along window cornices, and using the drapes like hanging vines. It was great fun, but not as much fun as their next activity. They discovered a food lift, or dumbwaiter, which transported dinner from the basement kitchen up to the dining room. Paul squeezed Connie into the lift and pulled on the rope. The pulley turned, and Connie disappeared up through the opening and into the wall. "I'm here," came back her muffled yell. Paul pulled the rope in the opposite direction to bring her back down.

Paul then climbed in to try it for himself. It was a slower trip up with Connie pulling on the rope, but he was fascinated to peek out of the cupboard door at the top and get a different view of the dining room. He felt sure this was the best way ever invented to get from one floor to the next, that is, until he spied the huge trays that Cissie used for baking bread. The trays were just too tempting not to try out on the carpeted stairs.

Paul and Connie each carried a baking tray to the top of the third-floor stairs. Paul was the first to set his tray down on the top step and sit on it. He pushed off and was soon on his way bumping down the stairs. When he reached the bottom of that flight, he scooted to the next flight of stairs and slid down them as well. It was all so much fun!

Suddenly Aunt Hope appeared. "What do you think you're doing, young man?" she demanded with a slight smile on her face.

Paul felt his face grow red, but he was glad that it was Aunt Hope who had caught him. Mama said that she sometimes raced down the stairs singing at the top of her voice, an unladylike thing to do.

"I think you'd better go and play outside until dinnertime," Aunt Hope said, picking up the trays. "I'll see that these get back to the kitchen where they belong."

Outside, the world was just as foreign to Paul as it was inside the house. It was hard to see more than a few houses down the street, and they all looked the same. Their exteriors were gray, the streets were gray, the weather was cold and gray. Paul longed for a bright, sunny day with the wind in his face, as he had been used to when he rode his father's horse through the fields of the Indian hill country. Still, he decided that he and Connie would just have to make do with what they had.

Paul surveyed the scene. He noted a gas lamppost outside of the house with a crossbar about twelve feet up. Climbing the post did not seem like a difficult challenge, and that is what he and Connie did. Soon they were swinging upside down from each side of the crossbar with their knees looped over it. Paul was delighted to see the shocked expressions on the faces of passersby as they looked up and saw the pair swinging there. It was the most fun he'd had since arriving in England.

By contrast, Sunday did not turn out to be much fun at all. It was then that Paul realized just how different life in London was going to be. Aunt Eunice explained to the children that Sunday was a special day set aside to worship and contemplate God. This was not new to Paul, who was used to setting out the mats in the chapel on Sunday back in India and listening to his father's sermons in Tamil. But a London Sunday was not nearly the same as an Indian one. It seemed to Paul that English Sundays revolved around what could and could not be done, worn, or touched.

On their first Sunday morning in the house the children were introduced to the drawing room. They were expected to sit quietly in the room while the adults drank tea and talked. Aunt Eunice gave them permission, if they were very careful, to look at but not touch some of the family treasures displayed there. Among the things on display were an opal from Australia, a small thimble made from a peach stone, a pair of carved ivory eggcups, brightly colored shells, and tiny salt and pepper shakers. Many of the items were very old and had been in the family a long time.

Aunt Eunice produced a box of blocks that had belonged to the Harris children when they were young. "You may play quietly with these," she told Paul and Connie, "as long as you build religious objects only."

Paul looked at her questioningly.

"For example, the Tabernacle or a Hebrew house," Aunt Eunice explained.

Paul decided that he could make just about anything and call it the Tower of Babel or the Temple of Solomon!

The following Saturday, Uncle Bertie was driving the Brand family forty miles southwest to Guildford, where Paul's father's family lived. As they rode, Jesse told the story of his family's long connection to India. Jesse's grandfather, Joseph Brand, had been the first member of the family to settle in India. He had never intended to live there, but as a young man he had enlisted as a midshipman. While on the ship, he had committed an offense and was arrested. When the ship was at anchor off Bombay, Joseph managed to escape from the vessel and swim to shore.

In Bombay Joseph got a job with a well-off merchant and eventually married the man's daughter. He became very wealthy during his time in Bombay and later decided to return to England with his family. He left his money in a Bombay bank and took with him a bag of jewels to fund his new life in England. However, the jewels were stolen before the family reached their destination. Soon after the family arrived in England, the bank in Bombay failed, and Joseph lost all of his money. Now his grandson, Jesse Brand, also called India home. But Jesse was not there to earn money and get rich. He was there to preach the gospel and use his medical and building skills to help the Indian people.

Once the travelers arrived at the family house in Guildford, Paul's father's five sisters and one brother and their families were waiting for them. Jesse was the oldest child, and Paul was overwhelmed with how happy all his father's siblings were to see him again.

It did not take Paul long to realize that the Brands were less strict than the Harrises. However, Paul and Connie managed to give their father's sister, Aunt Daisy, quite a fright. On Sunday morning Jesse was to preach at the local Baptist church. By now Paul knew that he had to dress in his most formal outfit, which included highly polished shoes, long socks, shorts, a shirt, a vest, and a jacket. Once they arrived at church, Paul was relieved to be able to take off his shoes and carry them down the aisle. Connie followed his lead.

"What are you doing?" Aunt Daisy hissed as she turned to see the children with their shoes in hand.

Paul registered the horrified look on his aunt's face but had no idea what he had done wrong, that is, until he looked around. *How extraordinary!* he thought. In the Kolli Hills everyone took off his or her shoes at the church entrance, but in England no one bothered to do so! Paul and Connie pulled their shoes back on.

Soon Jesse was off traveling farther afield to other churches in England, telling of the missionary work he was doing among the people of the Kolli Hills and raising money for a girls' home and school to be built there.

While Jesse was away, Paul and Connie and their mother stayed at the Harris home in London, where the children were enrolled in Miss Chattaway's small private school, within walking distance of the house.

After just one day at Miss Chattaway's, dressed in his itchy woolen shorts, striped tie, and domed cap, Paul longed for the freedom of his school in the tree. He daydreamed about sitting in his cotton shorts high up in the branches doing his math sums and lowering his book to his mother on a rope.

The hardest thing for Paul to get used to was being inside so much of the time. In winter the weather in London was cold and damp, and it was dark by three-thirty in the afternoon. How far away his life in India now seemed. Paul struggled to remember how much freedom he had enjoyed there. As he thought about life in India, he realized how different his life had been from the other boys in his class and how impossible it was to describe his experiences to them.

The year sped by, but in the back of his mind, Paul knew that when it was over his parents would be returning to India without him or Connie. Paul watched his mother paint plaques with Bible verses on them in English and Tamil. Evelyn hung several of them over Paul's bed and urged him to read them every night before he went to sleep and to think about what they meant to him.

The time arrived for Paul and Connie to say good-bye to their parents. It was a school day, so there was little time to linger in the morning. Paul and Connie got ready for school as usual and then knelt with their parents in the drawing room. Paul's mother and father prayed for their children and promised to write every week. Then they kissed Paul and Connie and hugged them.

Paul was the first to grab his schoolbag and head for the door, and Connie followed. The two of them ran down the steps, turned around once to wave, and disappeared around the corner and into a lane.

Paul could barely concentrate on his schoolwork that day as he thought about his parents leaving the house and embarking on a ship without him. He imagined his mother weeping as the ship cast off and his father putting a comforting arm around her.

That night was one of the loneliest in Paul's life. Nothing in the house seemed the same without his parents there. Even though Aunt Eunice and Aunt Hope were especially kind, Paul felt abandoned. Before he went to sleep, he studied a picture of himself and Connie and their parents standing by their home in the Kolli Hills. He propped the picture on his nightstand, where he could see its outline even in the darkened room. He recited the words on the plaques that his mother had painted: "I will be a father unto you" and "As one whom a mother comforteth, so will I comfort you." As he drifted off to sleep, Paul wondered how he was going to make it through the four years until he would see his parents again. He would be fourteen years old by then, and four years seemed an impossibly long way off.

Chapter 4

An English Boy

D ear Miss Harris," Aunt Eunice read aloud in an accusing tone. "We have not been too satisfied with young Brand of late. He is really a boy of good ability, and I feel that if he will wake up, he will do very well indeed."

Aunt Eunice paused for a moment, raised her eyebrows, and stared at Paul before she continued reading. "No doubt he is not yet used to our English climate. But he is often late and reads on the way to school. He ought to have a good talking to, both now and just before the beginning of the new term. Yours truly . . ."

"That was from your headmistress," Aunt Eunice snapped. "How am I supposed to explain that to your father and mother?"

Paul did not have the slightest idea how to answer the question. It was true that he struggled at school. So much of what he was taught didn't interest him. Paul would rather be outside exploring than crammed into a small, dark classroom listening to dull lessons. Of course, he did not think that he should say that to Aunt Eunice. She would just respond by telling him that he had to adjust, had to get used to being an English boy, and he could not spend his youth dreaming about India.

This was quite a problem, and Paul was glad that summer was on its way. Not only would school be closed, but also he could spend his days outside. He was going on holiday with Uncle Charlie's family and some other cousins to the seaside at West Runton on the east coast of England. Paul always enjoyed spending time with his uncle and his family. Unlike his aunts back at the house in London who were strict Baptists—too strict, Paul thought—Uncle Charlie, much to the chagrin of his older sisters, had become a Presbyterian. While still a devout Christian man, Uncle Charlie did not mind if Paul read books on Sunday and played outside.

The six-week vacation Paul spent at West Runton was just what he needed. He did not have to think about school, and he could spend his days doing all the things he liked. It reminded him of being back in India. He could take his shoes off, run, climb trees all he wanted, and read all day.

When Paul returned from his vacation in West Runton, a pile of letters was waiting for him. Several of the letters were from his father, who tended to do most of the letter writing. Paul's heart skipped as he picked up the envelopes. His father wrote such interesting letters, and these were no different. Paul opened the letters in the order they were dated. The most recent one was three months old by now.

"Remember the old Poosari at Kirangadu? Very old, first man to have a tooth out. One day last week he appeared and asked Mama if she would take an orphan baby. Mama could not believe her ears, so she brought the man to me." Paul smiled to himself as he read, remembering that his father spoke Tamil like a native while his mother struggled with the language. "He had a girl baby about a year old whose parents had both died, and he wanted us to take her. We told him to bring her along the next morning. He turned up with a lad carrying the baby, pretty, with large, dark eyes."

Paul could imagine the scene: his mother taking the little girl; the old man disappearing before she changed her mind; his mother bathing the baby in the bucket (the same one she and Paul had used to bathe so many sick children); his mother feeding the child rice and bananas and putting her to bed. Paul felt a sudden pang; perhaps the baby was sleeping in his bed.

The next letter demonstrated that Jesse Brand had received a letter from Aunt Eunice. Paul grimaced as he read. "The report that came this week, Paul, was a disappointing one. I don't mind low marks in some subjects, but what I object to is a remark like 'Could do better if he tried.'" Paul felt chastised by his father's remarks. He promised himself that he would do better at school when the new term began.

When school did start again, however, Paul fell into his old habit of studying only the things he enjoyed. He loved to read, and he marveled at all of the books so readily available to him. He read during lunch hour and after school. Unlike most of the other boys, he was not interested in organized sports, though one particular day everyone at school learned that Paul was as fit and coordinated as any of the institution's star sportsmen.

By now Paul had transferred from Miss Chattaway's private school to the junior branch of the University College School in nearby Hampstead. Given his love of climbing trees, Paul decided to try his hand at climbing up the brick and concrete corner post of the old school building. The boys gathered at the bottom to watch as inch by inch Paul worked his way up the outside of the building. When he was about forty feet up, Paul took out his locker key and, to the amazement of the other students, scratched his name into the concrete. He then scrambled back down to the ground. In the history of University College School, only one other student had managed to climb higher up the corner post of the building, but he had been unable to steady himself enough to scratch his name into the concrete.

As he grew, Paul searched for ways to stay connected to his parents' missionary work in India. One day he, Connie, and two of their cousins hit upon a great idea that would not only raise money for a new girls' home and school in India but also keep the family and church informed about what was going on there: they would create a newsletter.

The children titled the sixteen-page publication *The Superior Newsletter*. They wrote all of its content, which included poems, stories, puzzles, jokes, riddles, a section called "Tips and Gadgets", and, of course, news about what was happening with the Brands on the mission field in India. They wrote and designed the pages using pens with special ink. These pages were then used to make master pages in a film of gelatin, which in turn was used to print pages on a hectograph, or jelligraph, as it was more often called.

When they had produced a new edition of *The Superior Newsletter*, the children sold copies to family members and friends from church and sent the money they collected to Jesse and Evelyn Brand in India. Paul was proud of his contribution to the mission work of his parents. He was especially proud when he was able to announce in 1925 that the new girls' home and school had been completed. Now his mother had somewhere other than the family mission house in which to house all the young Indian girls she cared for.

Throughout each year that passed, Paul's parents continued to faithfully write and tell him about their missionary work in India. Jesse was busier than ever. Six mission stations workers were now spread across the Kolli Malai highlands. Jesse visited each

one regularly, as well as the ninety or so villages dotted around the mission stations. In one year alone he
preached over four thousand sermons.

Then there was the job of overseeing the girls'
home and school, not to mention Jesse's usual work
of providing medical care; teaching the locals about
agriculture and building; and teaching other practical
crafts, such as weaving, carpentry, and brickmaking.

Jesse had also set up a small loan cooperative
that loaned money to local farmers at affordable
rates. Until then, most farmers were forced to borrow money from lenders down on the plains, who
charged extremely high interest rates, usually 35 percent or more. Jesse also intervened in land and other
disputes on behalf of the people and usually found a
fair solution to the dispute.

People living in the Kolli Hills area had been
neglected by the government for years, and Jesse
decided to do something about it. He convinced the
government to put up the money to build all-weather
trails around the region. With the money, Jesse hired
local laborers and supervised the building of thirty
miles of horse trails.

As he read his parents' letters, Paul was proud
of what they were accomplishing in India. Paul's
mother seemed to keep as busy as his father. Not
only did she often travel with Jesse as he visited the
outlying villages and mission stations, but also she
cared for the girls in the home and school.

Despite the pride Paul felt in his parents' accom-
plishments, he missed them greatly and looked

forward to the following year when they would
return to England on furlough. Then one day in April
1929 he received a crushing blow. Only a few months
before his parents were due back in England, a letter arrived from them. Paul anxiously tore it open,
hoping to find out the exact date of their arrival, and
began reading the typed page. "We are disappointed
to give up our furlough this year," the letter began.
A lump formed in Paul's throat as he read on. "But
there is another man in the mission who needs it
more than we do. Looking forward to next year, we
think that the first week in March will be the prob-
able time of our setting sail. That will land us home
in time for the Easter holidays."

Another missionary needed rest and relaxation
more! And his parents had agreed to delay their furlough by one year so that the missionary could come
home instead! Paul could scarcely believe it, and he
tried to hide his sadness. He was now a fourteen-
year-old English boy, and he was not supposed to
show his emotions, but it was difficult not to let the
disappointment show of having to wait another year
to see his parents.

Paul distracted himself with new hobbies. He
delved into conducting scientific experiments, which
did not always go as planned. On one occasion he
was in the basement breakfast room boiling methyl
spirits in a can over a candle. He was hoping to cap-
ture the gas produced and use it to fuel a small camp
stove. But things went wrong. The tube he was using
to collect the gas melted, and the boiling methyl

spirits burst into flame and exploded from the can throughout the room. The maids rushed to Paul's aid and helped him put out the flames. They then forbade him to do any more science experiments in the basement.

Paul turned his attention to another activity—building and walking on stilts. He started small and became very adept at maneuvering them. Once he had mastered that art, he began making longer and longer stilts until he had made a pair that he had to climb onto from a first-floor window.

The summer holidays finally arrived, and Paul spent the first week exploring local parks and woodlands with his cousin Norman. It disappointed him to think that his parents were not there for the summer, but at least he was outside, roaming and exploring nature and enjoying the unusually warm summer.

On Saturday, June 15, 1929, Paul and Norman returned from a long walk in the park. As usual their bodies were dirty and scratched from climbing trees and crawling around under bushes looking for frogs and insects. As they approached the front door of the house, Aunt Eunice was waiting for them with a peculiar look on her face. "Norman, you had better go home now," she said. "Paul, come into the drawing room."

Paul and Norman gave each other confused looks and then parted ways. Whatever was going on, it must be serious, Paul reasoned, because Aunt Eunice was allowing him into the drawing room all scratched and dirty from the park. Paul was even more puzzled when he noticed Uncle Bertie standing quietly in the corner, his head bowed. What could possibly be the matter? He had done nothing seriously wrong, at least not that he could think of.

Chapter 5

Finding His Calling

Paul was unnerved by the strange tension in the drawing room. He noticed a crisp piece of yellow paper in Aunt Eunice's hand, the kind of paper telegrams were printed on. Aunt Eunice looked at Uncle Bertie, who cleared his throat and opened his mouth to speak. No words came out. Watching his normally talkative uncle so tongue-tied frightened Paul. Had something terrible happened?

Since his uncle was having trouble speaking, Aunt Eunice stepped in. "We're sorry to have to break the news so suddenly, Paul," she said softly, a quiver in her voice, "but your dear daddy has gone to be with Jesus."

Paul stood completely still while the world spun around him. Had he heard his aunt correctly? What

49

did it mean? Was his father really dead? It seemed too much to take in. He could hear his aunt continuing to talk but could not distinguish the words or take in what she was saying.

After what seemed like hours, Uncle Bertie walked over and picked his hat up from the table. "I am going to get Connie from Guildford. I will be back in a few hours," he said as he left the drawing room.

Meanwhile, Paul's two aunts sat him down and brought him a cup of tea. Paul drank it, unsure of what to do next. What was there to do? His forty-four-year-old father was dead from blackwater fever, a complication of malaria, but everything else in Paul's life was as it had been for the past six years. It had been that long since he and his father had been together.

Uncle Bertie arrived back at the house with Connie. Paul could tell immediately that his sister had been told the bad news. Connie's eyes were filled with panic.

"You children will want to be alone together," Aunt Eunice said, standing up. "You will have things to say to each other." With that she reached down, took Paul's elbow, and guided Paul and Connie upstairs to Paul's room, where she shut the door firmly behind them.

Paul stood stiffly, his sister beside him, but no words came.

Connie broke the silence. "It's dreadful, isn't it?"

"Yes, it is," Paul replied. "I just can't believe it." He could not think of anything to add, and neither could Connie. They continued standing together in silence for a while, and then Connie returned to her own room.

The days that followed were a blur of confusion for Paul. His father's weekly letters had been a lifeline. For a while letters Jesse had posted before his death continued to arrive each Friday. It gave Paul goose bumps to see his father's meticulous handwriting on each envelope, with the Indian postage stamp and franking date. As long as the letters continued coming, it was all the more difficult for Paul to believe that his father was really dead.

Although it was painful to do so, Paul read each letter that arrived. The last one, dated May 12, 1929, read, "When I am alone on these long rides, I just love the sweet smelling world, the dear brown earth, the lichen on the rocks, the heaps of dead brown leaves drifting like snow in the hollows. God means us to delight in his world. Just observe. Remember. Compare. And be always looking to God with thankfulness and worship."

It seemed a tall order for Paul to fulfill his father's wishes, especially since he was worried about his mother. He did not understand everything, but from what he could work out, the mission had a strict policy of sending a missionary wife home immediately if her husband died. But Evelyn Brand refused to leave her station. The Harris family was frantically trying to get her to come back to England. In the end it was decided that Paul's older cousin, Ruth Harris, who was in her last year of medical school, would take time off from her studies and go to India in the hope of talking sense into Evelyn. The ploy worked, and eventually Ruth cabled to say that she and Paul's mother had booked passage to England.

Paul waited eagerly for his mother's arrival. "Everything will be different when Mother gets here," he confidently told Connie. Their mother was strong, beautiful, and feisty. She would help them understand what had happened. On the train to the Tilbury docks to meet the ship, Paul was so impatient to see his mother again that he wished the train would go faster. When they arrived at the dock, the P&O ocean liner had already berthed, and passengers were flowing down the gangplank. Suddenly Uncle Bertie pointed. "There they are!" he exclaimed.

Paul could see Ruth Harris on the gangplank. Behind her was a tiny, shrunken woman he did not recognize. Paul wondered how his mother and Ruth had become separated disembarking the ship and continued to scan the other disembarking passengers for a glimpse of his mother.

Moments later, Ruth was embracing Uncle Bertie, and the woman who had been behind her fell into Connie's arms weeping. "Mother! Mother darling!" Connie sobbed.

Paul drew back at the sight. This woman was his mother? He wanted to run back to the train and hide. But before he could move, he felt himself being enveloped in a hug from Ruth and then being pushed gently toward his mother. Evelyn let out a cry, and threw her arms around her son. Paul dutifully kissed her on the cheek and then stepped back. His heart felt like stone.

The train ride home did not soften his heart. His mother sat between him and Connie. At first she plied the children with questions about their schooling and holidays. Paul answered her politely, as he would any stranger. Then Evelyn got a faraway look, and she began weeping. "I don't know how I will go on," she said. "Your papa was my entire life. I am not whole without him. All the light has gone out of my life. There is only darkness left. What am I going to do without him? I will never be the same."

Paul shrank back toward the carriage window, uncomfortable with his mother's public display of grief.

The next weeks and months were difficult for Paul, Connie, and their mother. Evelyn Brand would weep one minute and tell stories of how she could never again be a missionary, and then in the next breath, grab Paul's hand and tell him that she had to find a way to get back to the hill people in India— "Jesse's hill people," as she called them. At other times she begged Paul to grow up and follow in his father's footsteps. It was more than Paul could take. His mother disrupted his life so much that he almost wished she had not come back to England.

With everything that was going on at home, school receded farther into the background of Paul's life. In December 1930, sixteen-year-old Paul Brand decided that he was done with school. In the English school system, boys who did not have a lot of academic promise or who wanted to learn a trade left school at that age. Those who wanted to go on to university and professional jobs stayed for another year of schooling.

Even though Paul's mother urged him to stay in school and study to become a doctor, Paul had no interest in either staying in school or joining the medical profession. Sometimes he struggled to bring back specific memories of his father, but the one memory that was always close was that of his father draining pus from the infected leg of an Indian man. He could still conjure up the sickening stench of the pale yellow pus oozing into the bucket.

"No, thank you!" Paul told his mother. "Medicine is not the life for me."

Paul wanted to do something more practical that did not involve a lot more schoolwork. In the end he chose to follow in his father's and grandfather's footsteps and become a builder. Soon he was apprenticed to Mr. Warwick, a devout Baptist who had known his father and under whose tutelage Paul would learn the craft of building houses.

On Monday, December 8, 1930, Paul entered an entirely new world—the world of the apprentice builder. He woke up at five-thirty in the morning so that he could eat breakfast, take an hour-long train ride across London, and be on the job by seven-thirty. In entering this new world, he also had to learn a new language—Cockney slang, which almost all the tradesmen and other apprentices on the job spoke. It was quite a change from the refined English he had learned growing up in West London. Still, he did not mind; more than anything else he wanted to fit in.

Being an apprentice was a five-year commitment that involved learning everything about a particular craft from a master tradesman. Paul was soon learning all the facets of building houses, including how to estimate the cost according to the plans, how to order the required amount of materials, and how to actually build the house. He also learned how to use tools, hammer in nails straight and true, put on roof tiles, and fit windows and doors so they were level and watertight.

Soon after Paul began his building apprenticeship, his mother managed to persuade the mission board to take the unusual step of allowing her to return to the Kolli Hills region of India to serve as a missionary once again.

During the next five years Paul worked diligently to become a builder. In his spare time he played tennis, taught Sunday school, and organized youth meetings. He also made many new Christian friends.

In 1935 Paul finished his building apprenticeship and was ready to take the next step in life. By now his mother was back in London, and she urged him to think of the unsaved millions of people in India. Paul listened to all she had to say and decided to take up the challenge and apply to a Baptist missionary society to be sent to India as a missionary builder.

Paul was shocked when the society turned him down, saying that they needed trained missionaries, not builders. The director of the mission society told

Paul that he would have to consider either going to
Bible college or taking a one-year course in tropical
medicine. Paul was reluctant to consider medicine.
He could still vividly remember the bucket of pus,
but as he prayed about the situation, he felt that taking the one-year medical course was the right thing
to do.

With little enthusiasm Paul walked through the
doors of the Livingstone Medical School in Leyton,
East London, the same medical school where his
father had received his education in tropical medicine. Paul hoped the year would pass quickly and
that he would have the attention span to take in all
of the detailed information. He expected the course
to be difficult, and it was, but he did not expect it
to be fascinating. Somehow, watching his father perform limited medical procedures back in India had
convinced Paul that medicine was all about blood
and pus and ulcers. To his amazement, he found that
it was about causes and cures, alleviating pain, and
treating ill people with dignity.

The year at tropical medicine school flew by. While
he studied, Paul stayed involved in his youth work
and often co-led events with David Wilmshurst, a fellow student and friend. The only sad note during the
year was the death of his Grandmother Harris at the
age of ninety-four.

At the end of the year, Paul and David were
among the top five students in the tropical medicine
course. It was not wholly unexpected when Paul was
called into the office of Dr. Wigram, the director of
the Livingstone Medical School.

"Ah, Brand, you like medicine, don't you?" Dr. Wigram began.

"I don't think *like* is the right word," Paul replied. "I love it!"

"Yes, I can certainly see you do," Dr. Wigram said. "In fact, my advice to you is to make medicine your profession."

"Become a doctor?" Paul questioned. "But I am planning to become a missionary."

"I know you are. But haven't you ever heard of a missionary doctor?" Dr. Wigram inquired.

"But it would take six years to become a doctor."

"Quite right. But all worthwhile things take time," Dr. Wigram said.

"But I have to get to the mission field," Paul said, stunned at the turn of events.

Undeterred, Dr. Wigram went on to explain to Paul that he had already contacted his mother, who had informed him that Paul's Uncle Dick had once promised to fund Paul's medical studies. Dr. Wigram, a step ahead of Paul, explained that he had already contacted Paul's uncle, who was still willing to fund Paul's medical studies.

Paul felt conflicted. Yes, he loved medicine, but he had chosen the path to go to the mission field as a builder as soon as possible. He felt that was what he must do, despite his Uncle Dick's generous offer to fund his medical studies. He had fulfilled the mission society's requirements to become a missionary, and he had expected to be in India sooner rather than later. Paul was encouraged in his decision when his friend David also was urged by Dr. Wigram to go on to medical school. David rejected the idea and made plans to set out for Africa.

The board of the mission society was pleased with how well Paul had done at the Livingstone Medical School. However, it felt that he still needed some Bible training before being sent to India. It suggested that Paul take the two-year course at a place called the Missionary Training Colony—the Colony, as most people referred to it.

The Colony was located in Norwood, Surrey, on the outskirts of London. It was designed to give prospective missionaries intensive Bible study and preaching practice, as well as a taste of the sparse lifestyle they would encounter on the mission field. Four large huts, each sleeping twelve, housed the Colony students. Paul was assigned to the Africa hut, where he had a bed, small desk, and straight-backed chair. The hut was heated by a charcoal stove, which Paul soon discovered was inadequate.

Despite the living conditions, Paul enjoyed life at the Colony. Each morning the students rose before daybreak and, regardless of the weather, jogged to a nearby park, where they did calisthenics before returning to their huts for cold baths. During the summer they undertook a six-hundred-mile trek through the Welsh and Scottish countryside, pulling all their supplies in a cart behind them. Paul also enjoyed the intense Bible study and the many opportunities to go into London to preach in the parks and on the streets.

All was proceeding well for Paul at the Colony until he came down with a bad case of influenza. He could not be sure whether the sickness muddled his mind or made his thoughts clearer. Either way, he felt certain his calling was not to be a Bible teacher or a missionary builder. He realized he had made a terrible mistake when he turned down the opportunity to become a doctor and help sick people. As he lay in bed sweating out the fever, Paul wondered whether his Uncle Dick might still be willing to fund his medical studies to become a doctor, providing he could pass the entrance examinations.

Chapter 6

Doctor in Training

"Thank You, God!" Paul exclaimed as he read the acceptance letter. He had made it into the University College Medical School, and his Uncle Dick had agreed to pay for his room and board and tuition. For the first time in many years, Paul felt like he was on track. He packed up the few belongings he had brought with him to the Colony and in early September 1937 moved to 49 Highbury Park, London, a hostel that housed twenty young men all studying to be doctors. Twenty-three-year-old Paul felt invigorated and ready to begin this entirely new phase of his life. Although he had moved only a few miles across London, Paul had entered another world. The Spartan lifestyle, Christian training, and camaraderie of the Colony were behind him, and ahead lay six years of study to achieve his goal of becoming a doctor.

The first thing Paul did after settling into medical school was to join the Student Union and make contact with other Christians in the program. The second thing he did was sign up for the University Squadron, where students would learn to fly in readiness for being called up to fight in a war. All of the students recognized that a dark cloud loomed over them—the dark cloud of a possible war in Europe. Even though newly elected British Prime Minister Neville Chamberlain was promising to "bring peace in our time" to Europe, many had their doubts that the Nazis in Germany in particular could be trusted, despite the prime minister's desire to negotiate peace in Europe with them. To his disappointment, Paul learned that medical students at the university were barred from signing up for the squadron. He was informed that their effort and skill would be needed in hospitals if war broke out. Paul was left to concentrate fully on his medical studies. In the case of war, there would be no flying in his future.

Later that week Paul headed to his first chemistry lab. Everyone in the lab sat in alphabetical order. Paul Brand and Margaret Berry were assigned to the same worktable. Paul introduced himself to the pretty, blonde woman sitting across from him, noting how young she looked. The two chatted as they performed their first lab assignment. Paul learned that Margaret, at seventeen years of age, had earned herself a full scholarship to medical school. He was impressed.

Margaret had a slight accent. She explained to Paul that she had been born in England but raised in South Africa, where her father had taken a job as a public health doctor. Paul was glad to find someone else in the class who had spent some of her childhood living in an exotic, faraway place. He told Margaret about his parents being missionaries in India and how he had been born there and spent the first nine years of his life in the hill country of southeast India. Margaret then volunteered that her older sister Anna had encouraged her to join the Christian Union.

"That's wonderful!" Paul exclaimed, remembering the prayer meeting he was going to attend when class was over. "Would you like to come along to the PM after class?" he asked.

Margaret's face lit up. "A PM? Of course, I would love to come."

When chemistry lab was over, Paul walked with Margaret to the meeting room, where several students were already on their knees praying. Margaret stood at the door frowning. "Didn't you say we were going to a PM?" she asked quizzically.

"Of course," Paul replied. "Doesn't this look like a *prayer meeting* to you?"

Margaret laughed out loud. "I guess we do come from different backgrounds. I thought you invited me to a *postmortem!*"

The relationship did not get off to a great start, not that Paul imagined its going very far anyway. He had no intention of dating any one person. He had too many other things to do, including study. And there, Margaret turned out to be a great help. She was ambitious and studious and had already finished

the chemistry class the previous year at a polytechnic school, but she was too young to take the exam
and get credit for the course. So now she was taking
the class again and offered to help Paul study. The
arrangement worked perfectly, and Paul received
the second highest exam grade in the eighty-member
class. Margaret beat him by several points to come in
first.

Paul was happy to report his grades to his mother,
who was preparing to return to India. Once again his
mother had persuaded the mission board to allow
her one more term of missionary service in India.
However, the board had adamantly refused to send
her back to the Kolli Hills region. Instead, she was
headed for Sendamangalam, on the plains, where
Paul's cousin, Dr. Ruth Harris, ran a busy medical
clinic and drove a mobile clinic to surrounding villages. Evelyn would be Ruth's new assistant.

The start of Paul's third year of medical school was
interrupted when clouds of war became a storm. On
September 1, 1939, Nazi Germany invaded Poland,
and Europe braced itself for what could come next.
Prime Minister Neville Chamberlain issued an ulti-
matum to Germany to immediately withdraw its
troops from Poland. When the Nazis ignored his ulti-
matum, Chamberlain declared Great Britain to be at
war with Germany on September 3, 1939.

Everyone in London scrambled to collect govern-
ment-issued gas masks and locate shelter from possible air raids. At night, outside lights had to be turned

off and windows blacked out so as not to make London an easy target for German Luftwaffe bombers.

People also made preparations inside their homes. Paul helped his aunts store supplies in the basement. One time when he visited Margaret's home in Northwood, on the outskirts of London, he got to try out a Morrison shelter that her father had arranged to be installed in the house. This was a sturdy, metal cage-like affair that the family could crawl into in case of a bombing attack. The shelter was reinforced so as to remain effective even if the upper floors of the house collapsed onto it.

Despite such preparations, everything seemed to go on pretty much as normal for Paul. There were air raid sirens and drills, but no German bombs. Nonetheless, the British government decreed that all pregnant women, children, and nonessential persons to the war effort should evacuate from London in advance of any attack. Children of all ages, with labels on their lapels, were hastily bundled into trains and transported into the countryside, where strangers took them in for the duration of the war.

The students at the University College Medical School were designated as nonessential persons, and the entire staff and student body evacuated the city. The men were moved to Cardiff, Wales, and the women to Sheffield in north central England.

Paul and three other students found board with an old Welsh woman, Mrs. Morgan, who lived in Llandaff, a village just outside Cardiff. Mrs. Morgan was a devout Christian, and when she learned that Paul's mother was serving as a missionary in India, she refused to take his weekly board money.

Paul was glad that he had lived with his two unmarried aunts in London for so long, because it helped him adjust to living with the eccentric old widow. Mrs. Morgan was completely deaf without the aid of a huge ear trumpet. Paul found it disconcerting when she held the trumpet to his chin so that she could hear what he was saying. Mrs. Morgan was also afraid of being bombed out of her home and so took to wearing several layers of clothes and hiding in the various layers of pockets important items such as her family Bible, house keys, papers, glasses, spare ear trumpet, and ration books. When she walked down the street, Mrs. Morgan rattled from all the things she was carrying.

Life in Cardiff settled into a busy but uncomplicated routine. Paul continued his medical studies at Cardiff University, where he completed his senior project—tracing the twelve cranial nerves that bypass the spinal cord and connect directly to the brain. These nerves link the sense organs of the head—the nose, eyes, mouth, and ears—to the brain. To accomplish this task, he was given the head of a cadaver to dissect. For the next month he carefully cut away flesh and chiseled off layers of bone as he traced the white, stringlike lines of nerves back into the brain. His professor was so impressed with Paul's painstaking work that he had the dissected head of the cadaver preserved and placed in a specimen jar on public display in the Welsh National School of Medicine Museum.

While living in Cardiff, Paul gave Mrs. Morgan his ration book, which entitled him each week to purchase one egg, egg powder, four ounces of meat, two rations of bacon, two ounces of butter, four ounces of margarine, half a pound of sugar, and half a pound of jam. With this and the rations from the other boarders, Mrs. Morgan made meals for them all. Because gasoline was also rationed, trips beyond Llandaff and Cardiff were rare. During his time in Wales, Paul studied hard, attended church and prayer meetings, and, like millions of other English men and women, tuned in to the BBC on the radio each night at 9:00 PM to hear the latest war news.

By May 1940 things were looking grim. To this point Paul had to admit that the war had been more of a nuisance than anything else. That all changed on May 10, when Nazi forces simultaneously invaded Holland, Belgium, and Luxembourg. Paul listened on the radio to the news of the attack and wondered what would happen next. Events started to accelerate. Holland, Belgium, and Luxembourg were overrun by German forces. By late May a huge contingent of British, French, and Belgian troops were trapped at the port of Dunkirk in northern France, close to the Belgian border. On the following evenings over the radio, Paul learned of the daring evacuation of the trapped soldiers in the face of the advancing Germans. A flotilla made up of almost every kind of boat imaginable, from ships to small pleasure boats, had crossed the English Channel to Dunkirk and begun evacuating the soldiers. It took a week, but by June 4, 1940, over 338,000 troops had been evacuated.

The days were dark for the British, and more so when the Nazis overran France. The English felt isolated and alone, yet resolved to fight to the bitter end. Everyone knew it was only a matter of time before the Germans launched an all-out attack on Great Britain. That attack began in July 1940, when waves of German Luftwaffe airplanes began bombing England. At first the Germans launched daylight bombing runs, attacking aircraft factories, airfields, and ports, mostly in the south of the country, in the hope of destroying the Royal Air Force.

Just as the German bombing of England began, Paul's time in Cardiff came to an end. It was time for Paul to return to London to begin his practical training at the University College Hospital. Paul studied surgical techniques at the hospital by day, took a brief nap before dinner, and then got up to care for the wounded and dying who were carried or hobbled into the hospital as a result of the German bombing. One of the recurring injuries Paul dealt with was Royal Air Force pilots whose faces had been burned. This occurred because of a design flaw in the Hurricane airplanes the pilots flew. The fuel lines threaded their way through the cockpit on the way to the engine mounted at the front of the plane. When these planes were hit, the cockpit would erupt in an intense, fuel-fed fireball. In the two or three seconds that it took the pilot to eject from his aircraft, the fire burned away his face. It was not uncommon for Paul to see pilots brought in with their noses, eyelids, lips, even their cheeks burned off. When a burned pilot arrived, Paul would help to stabilize his condition and prepare him for surgery. A talented team of plastic surgeons then set to work to reconstruct the pilot's facial features. Sometimes this would take as many as forty surgeries, with the surgeons often developing new techniques as they went. Paul was amazed at the results they could achieve.

In early September 1940, the Germans changed tactics. They switched to night bombing raids and focused on mercilessly bombing London. Night after night, loads of German bombs rained down on the city. Some of the city's residents sought shelter in underground railway tunnels. Others stayed in their homes and hoped and prayed that their homes would be spared.

The operating rooms at University College Hospital were transferred to the basement of the hospital so that the doctors would not be disturbed by anything less than a direct hit from a bomb. Every night Paul headed down to the basement and all the human misery it contained. As the stream of bombing victims rolled in, he was kept busy setting broken bones, giving blood transfusions, and cleaning, suturing, and bandaging wounds.

On one occasion Paul, with several other medical personnel, was called to the Imperial Hotel, where a bomb had hit the hotel's Turkish bathhouse. When he arrived, Paul found naked, dazed men standing and lying around in pools of blood, their flesh shredded by shards of glass from the shattered bathhouse windows. Paul set to work cleaning and suturing cuts on the spot and dispatching those who needed more intensive care to the hospital. The bodies of the dead were carried away.

On another night, as Paul was taking a rest on the hospital roof, he watched in horror as a bomb exploded on the roof of the infant ward at nearby Royal Free Hospital. The roof collapsed, and Paul raced to the scene to help with the rescue. He took his place in line as the living and dead bodies of small children were removed from the rubble and moved to safety.

The work was grueling as night after night Paul dealt with people with broken or severed limbs or who had suffered jagged cuts from flying shards of glass. Some had been crushed by collapsing buildings. Paul learned how to deal with each new emergency.

Paul discovered that he was particularly interested in hand injuries, and there were lots of them. Some people had their hands cut to shreds by glass and other flying material, while the hands of others were pulverized by falling wood and bricks. Paul marveled at the integrity of the hand, the way it was formed, and how perfectly all of the muscles, tendons, bones, and nerves worked together to create the movements that most people took for granted.

Whole sections of London were laid waste by the ceaseless German bombing. The British government eventually decided that all medical students should be evacuated from the city. The students were worth too much to the war effort to stay in harm's way. Paul was assigned to a hospital in Watford to the west of London. Meanwhile, Margaret Berry and some of the other female students were sent to Cardiff. Margaret stayed with Mrs. Morgan at Paul's suggestion.

Sometimes when he had time off, Paul would persuade a friend to take him to Cardiff by motorbike. Even this took a lot of organizing, since gasoline was strictly rationed. He told himself that he was going to check up on Mrs. Morgan, but once there, he seemed to spend more and more time with Margaret.

At the beginning of 1942 the war was still going strong, though the nightly bombing of London and other British cities was no longer as intense as it had been. Paul was doing his obstetrics training when he learned that Margaret was returning to London to do her emergency room training. The students all thought that was ironic, since they had already seen more than their share of medical emergencies.

One night after a Christian Medical Students' meeting, Paul walked Margaret home. It was a foggy night. Blackout conditions were in effect, and only faint lights flickered from the few cars that had gas and a reason to be out on the road. As they walked together, Paul found himself reaching for Margaret's hand.

Chapter 7

Mister Brand

As 1942 began to unfold, the state of the war and concern about his future weighed heavily on Paul. In December 1941, Japan had attacked Pearl Harbor, bringing the United States into the war alongside Great Britain and her allies. It had been a great morale boost to many in England to know that America was now fighting on their side, yet Great Britain was still in a precarious situation. The Germans continued their night bombing raids over English cities, though more intermittently than before. Many British people still believed that Hitler had his sights set on invading England.

It seemed increasingly likely that Paul would be called up to serve in the military once he completed his medical instruction. Because Paul was a doctor in training, the Central Medical War Committee of the British Medical Association, in cooperation with the War Department, had deferred his military service. But when his training was over, Paul would be required to spend two years serving in the military. Despite the uncertainty, Paul was sure about one thing: whatever happened next in his life, he wanted Margaret Berry at his side.

On a beautiful spring morning in 1942, Paul and Margaret were walking in the bluebell woods near Margaret's parents' home in Northwood. As they stopped to rest and sat side by side atop a farm gate, the words tumbled out of Paul's mouth. "Assuming one or the other of us gets called by God to serve Him in some other country, we shall go together. So, will you marry me?"

Paul realized that this was not the most romantic of marriage proposals, but he was delighted when Margaret beamed at him and answered, "Of course!"

When Paul and Margaret returned home from their walk, Paul formally asked Dr. Berry for Margaret's hand in marriage. Good wishes were conveyed all around, and a few tears were shed. It was a difficult time to be planning any new venture, and it took a lot of faith for Paul to believe that everything would go well.

For the most part, things did work out. In May 1943, Paul and Margaret both graduated as doctors from the University College Medical School. A week later, on May 29, Dr. Paul Brand and Dr. Margaret

Berry were married. Paul was twenty-eight years old, and Margaret was twenty-three. It had been six years since the two of them had been brought together at the worktable in their first chemistry lab by virtue of their "B" surnames.

The wedding was a modest affair held at Emmanuel Anglican Church in Northwood. One of Margaret's father's patients donated her clothing ration for the year so that Margaret could buy fabric for a wedding dress. Paul's sister Connie, who was in missionary training herself, and Paul's cousin Nancy wore borrowed bridesmaids dresses, and Paul's aunts gave him his Grandmother Harris's wedding ring to use during the ceremony. Paul's family showed up in force, including his uncles and aunts and numerous cousins, but his mother could not make it to the event. Evelyn was still in India, experiencing her own turmoil of war.

The newlyweds enjoyed a weeklong honeymoon in the Wye Valley on the border between England and Wales. Both Paul and Margaret were exhausted from their last year at medical school and found the week away restful. During their final year of medical school, both had chosen to combine their studies with internships so that upon graduation they could go straight into medical practice.

Following the honeymoon, Paul and Margaret had to consider their next step. Now that he was a trained doctor, Paul had two paths before him. His military deferment was over, so he could either serve the required two years in the military as a doctor or undertake postgraduate medical training, in which case the Central Medical War Committee would extend his deferment. As a female, Margaret, on the other hand, would have to serve in the military only if she could not find a medical job at home.

After much prayer and discussion about the situation, the newlyweds decided that Margaret would live at her parents' home in Northwood and join her father in his general medical practice. Meanwhile, Margaret's father urged Paul to continue his medical studies, working to become a surgeon. At first Paul was reluctant, but Dr. Berry persuaded him that the two extra years of study would be worth it for a talented doctor like him. The couple decided that while Margaret lived at home with her parents in Northwood and practiced medicine with her father, Paul would stay in London and work in the hospital while pursuing becoming a Fellow of the Royal College of Surgeons. The decision was difficult for Paul, especially since it meant that he and Margaret would see each other only two weekends a month.

Meanwhile, Paul's sister Connie had begun corresponding with David Wilmhurst, Paul's classmate from the Livingstone Medical School. In what seemed no time at all, Connie announced that she and David had fallen in love while writing to each other and that she was sailing to Africa to marry him and assist him in his missionary work. Paul was envious of her freedom to make such a quick decision. He and Margaret longed to be on the mission field themselves, but he had an obligation to the Central Medical War

Committee to serve in the armed forces, and there seemed no way out of that for him.

Paul went back to University College Hospital in London as a house surgeon. The night bombings continued, and the wounded still poured into the hospitals. During the day Paul assisted in routine surgeries on such things as clubfoot and inborn hip dislocations, and at night he treated bombing victims. Sometimes as he worked, he was so tired that he hardly knew what he was doing.

One morning as he was making his rounds of the hospital wards, Paul noticed that someone had prescribed a new drug to one of his patients. He called the nurse over. "Who signed off on this medication?" he asked.

She looked at him quizzically. "Why, you did, Dr. Brand—last night after you were done with the casualties."

Paul picked up the chart again and ran his finger down it. Sure enough, there was his signature next to the new medication. He stepped back shocked. He had no recollection of being in that ward the previous night. Paul knew that he desperately needed a break, but when he looked around the hospital, he realized that everyone else working in the place did too. It was the nature of a long war to push everyone to his or her physical and mental limits.

Paul's life was about to get more complicated. On one of his visits to Margaret, she announced that she was expecting a baby in March the following year. It was hardly the best of times to be having a baby, but

Paul was grateful for a new life, and he prayed that Margaret would stay safe and healthy.

Early in 1944, Paul became the Resident Surgical Officer at the Hospital for Sick Children on Great Ormond Street, London. Here he seemed to be busier than he had been at University College Hospital. Nonetheless, when he was informed on March 8, 1944, that Margaret had gone into labor, he rushed to the Royal Northern Hospital, where they had agreed she would deliver the baby.

When Paul got to the hospital, the doctor informed the couple that Margaret still had a long time to wait before delivery of the baby. Paul had a cup of tea with his wife and returned to Great Ormond Street Hospital to resume his schedule. He waited and prayed for the rest of the day, but no word came on Margaret's progress on giving birth.

That night Paul took his turn on fire watch atop the eight-story hospital building. His heart sank as he surveyed the night sky above London. It was a moonlit night, and flares of bright orange lit up the sky as bombed buildings burned to the east, sending plumes of acrid, black smoke into the air. It was all Paul could do not to leave his post and race over to the Royal Northern Hospital to be with Margaret. He managed to stay on the roof until his watch was over, and then he climbed down the stairs and back into the carnage of bombing victims coming through the hospital doors.

With no news yet from Margaret, Paul flopped into his bed at the hospital. He was so tired he fell into a deep sleep. When he awoke several hours later, he noticed a slip of paper on his nightstand. It read, "To inform you that you are the father of a bonny, bouncing boy."

Paul jumped out of bed and dressed in record time. He took a bus across town and was relieved when the Royal Northern Hospital came into sight. The building had not been bombed during the night, but as the bus got closer, Paul noticed that the hospital had been cordoned off. He got off the bus, his heart pounding, and went to see what the problem was. He learned that several bombs had been dropped during the night in the vicinity of the hospital but had not exploded. Now they had to be defused and removed before it was safe for anyone to enter the hospital grounds.

Paul waited with the other visitors and patients at the hospital until the way was clear for him to go inside and find Margaret. She was exhausted from a long labor, but the baby, whom they were going to name Christopher, was fine and healthy. As he picked up the newborn child, Paul could hardly believe that he had a son.

Following their release from the hospital, Margaret and Christopher went back to live with Margaret's parents. Margaret's sister, Anna, and her baby daughter, Ruth, also lived at the house, as Anna's husband, Anthony, was serving in the military.

Since everything in England and in their lives seemed to revolve around the war, Paul and Margaret prayed that it would soon end. They still wanted to be missionaries, but there was no way this was possible during wartime.

Paul continued with his busy schedule at the hospital and with the rigorous course of study required for him to become a surgeon. In May 1945 he passed his final exam. Now, as was the custom in the medical profession in England, he could be called by the title Mister Brand, rather than just Dr. Brand, and he could put FRCS (Fellow of the Royal College of Surgeons) after his name.

Paul and Margaret, along with the rest of the population of Great Britain, received the wonderful news in early May that the war in Europe was over. Hitler was dead, and Germany had surrendered. This news was followed three months later by the news that Japan also had surrendered. World War II was finally over.

Despite the war being over, the Central Medical War Committee still required Paul to complete his two years of military service, which had been deferred as he studied to become a doctor and then a surgeon. Paul thought that most likely he would be called up to serve with the Royal Air Force, probably somewhere in Asia.

Meanwhile, after ten years away, Paul's mother arrived back in England on furlough. She had never met Margaret, and when she did, Paul noted that she seemed glad that his wife's hair was naturally wavy. Granny Brand, as Evelyn was now called, confessed that upon seeing the wedding photos she had assumed that Margaret had a permanent wave in her hair. To

Paul's mother this meant "worldly," and worldly was not what she approved of in a daughter-in-law.

Once that issue had been sorted out, Margaret, Paul, and his mother all got along well. It was helpful that Paul's mother was there to shed light on the strange telegram Paul received from India: "There is urgent need for a surgeon to teach at Vellore. Can you come on short-term contract? Cochrane."

Paul could not imagine who Cochrane was, and he only vaguely remembered hearing about Vellore. How had Cochrane even found his name and where he lived? Paul went straight to his mother to find out what she knew about Vellore and this Cochrane person.

Chapter 8

Vellore

Paul looked directly at his mother. "Do you know why I would get a telegram inviting me to work at Vellore?" he asked. "If I remember correctly, that's a Christian hospital in southern India, isn't it?"

His mother nodded enthusiastically. "What a wonderful opportunity!" she exclaimed.

"Yes," Paul said, "but how do they even know I exist?"

Evelyn folded her hands and sat up straight in her chair. "Well, I did pass through Vellore on my way back to England, and I might have told Dr. Cochrane that my son had just earned his Royal College of Surgeons credentials. You know, Paul, it's a wonderful hospital. It would be perfect for you and Margaret. If the Lord wants you there, of course," she added.

Paul sighed. "That's not really the point at the moment. It's pretty much impossible. There's no way the Central Medical War Committee is going to let me out of my two years of military service. Besides, I've only just qualified as a surgeon. I don't have the experience for the job. And last but not least, with another baby on the way, Margaret needs me."

Evelyn nodded, but Paul did not think she had taken to heart any of his excuses for not going. Paul got a similar response from Margaret when he told her about the telegram. "You want to go, don't you?" she responded with a smile.

"It's impossible," Paul explained, beginning to think that he was the only person looking at the reality of the situation. "For one thing, we are having another baby."

"No, Paul, *I'm* having a baby," Margaret corrected him, "and I dare say it will come whether you are here in London, in the Royal Air Force, or in India."

"There's a lot more to it than that," Paul retorted. "Besides, the Central Medical War Committee will never release me from my military service," he added with a note of finality.

The following day Paul composed a letter to Dr. Cochrane in Vellore, outlining the reasons why it would be impossible for him to come to India. Six weeks later, Paul received a response from Dr. Cochrane, who would be in London the following Friday and wanted to meet Paul under the clock at Victoria Station at noon.

Paul sighed when he read the letter. He did not really have time to meet with the doctor, and now he would have to explain to this man that the situation was completely out of his hands. Nonetheless, the following Friday Paul waited under the clock at Victoria Station, more out of courtesy than anything else. In the intervening days Paul had recalled once meeting Dr. Robert Cochrane years before. Dr. Cochrane, a Scotsman and one of the foremost leprosy specialists in the world, had come to give a lecture at the Livingstone Medical School while Paul was a student there. When the doctor showed up at Victoria Station a few moments later, Paul marveled. Robert Cochrane hardly seemed to have aged a day since that time at the Livingstone Medical School.

Paul and the doctor shook hands and exchanged pleasantries before Dr. Cochrane came straight to the point. He explained how the Vellore Christian Medical College and Hospital was being upgraded to meet new medical standards put in place in India. The college and hospital had been established in 1900 to train and equip Indian women as doctors and nurses. New buildings were now being added to provide more teaching beds in the hospital, and the medical college had been enlarged and opened up to men. All of this was happening fast to meet the government's schedule for change, and with the expansion, there was an urgent need for qualified surgeons and teachers to come to Vellore.

"I need you. We must have you there," Dr. Cochrane declared.

Paul explained to Dr. Cochrane that as flattered as he was by the offer, he could not accept the position. For one, he had to serve two years in the British armed forces. Plus, his wife was having another baby. And he had only just qualified as a Fellow of the Royal College of Surgeons. He had barely two years' experience in the surgical field, not the eight or nine years' experience needed for a teaching post.

Dr. Cochrane listened to Paul's list of excuses and brushed them aside one by one. "As to your military service, leave that to me," he explained. "As to your qualifications to teach, let me be the judge of that. I know your record, and it is quite remarkable. And Vellore is a wonderful place for your wife and children."

Paul was impressed by Dr. Cochrane's tenacity, but he doubted that the doctor could persuade the Central Medical War Committee to allow Paul to forgo his two years of military service. Paul left their meeting feeling rather depressed. *What a pity,* he thought as he boarded the train. *This would be a wonderful opportunity if only circumstances were different, but there's really no way this can work out.*

Two weeks later an official envelope arrived in the mail for Paul from the Central Medical War Committee. Paul opened the letter with trepidation, expecting it to be his call-up papers for military service. Instead, the first words that caught his eye on the page inside were "Exempted from service." Paul scanned the document until his eyes fixed on "Free to leave the country." As he read the words, tears sprung to his eyes. Somehow Dr. Cochrane had pulled off the unthinkable—Paul was released from his military service deferment.

Despite this good news, Margaret was still having their second child, and Paul was still very inexperienced for the teaching job. Yet in his heart Paul began to believe that this was the path God wanted him to follow. He prayed with Margaret, and together they decided that Paul should head for India and that Margaret and the two children would follow him there when she felt strong enough.

The contrast between the reaction of Paul's mother and that of Margaret's parents could not have been starker. "Stottherum!" ("Praise God" in Tamil) declared Evelyn Brand as she expressed how excited she was that her son was returning to India. She herself had just finished negotiating with the mission board, and the board was allowing her to go back to India for one more term.

The Berrys, on the other hand, were visibly upset by the news. They had heard Margaret and Paul talk about missionary life many times, but they believed having two children would settle them down into a normal English life. "Surely you can see there are plenty of people in England who need the gospel," Margaret's mother pleaded. "Why would you want to take little children so far away? They could catch any number of tropical diseases."

Paul knew their concern was real. He was no stranger to the notion of death in a foreign land. His own father had succumbed to blackwater fever. Despite the concerns, Paul felt sure that Vellore was the next step for his growing family. However, he did have some concerns. What if he died in India and left his own son Christopher fatherless? And, he was scheduled to depart from England in the first week of November. What if Margaret hadn't had the baby by then or had a difficult childbirth or even lost the child? Wouldn't she need him at home by her side? They were unanswerable questions, and Paul tried to put them aside. If God was calling him to India, He would take care of the details.

Even so, it was difficult for Paul to begin packing. A very pregnant Margaret sat at the end of the bed watching while two-year-old Christopher crawled around on the bedroom floor. Paul hoped that the new baby would arrive before his scheduled departure date.

He was grateful that on October 18, 1946, Jean Brand was born. Paul was delighted to be the father of a little girl, and he knew that the two weeks he would have with the child before his departure would be precious.

When the time came to leave, Paul hated saying good-bye to Margaret and the children. It bought back memories of saying good-bye to his own father all those years ago. He hoped it would not be long before Margaret and the children joined him in Vellore.

Paul sailed away from England and retraced the voyage he had made from India to England as a nine-year-old. The three-week journey included passage down the Atlantic Coast of Europe, across the Mediterranean Sea, and through the Suez Canal.

After twenty-three years away, Paul was back in India, the land of his birth. He could hardly believe it as he stepped from the ship and breathed in the smells and took in the sights of the streets crowded with people and vendors. In an instant his childhood came rushing back to him. What many would consider chaos seemed natural and normal to Paul. To him, everything was as it should be, as it was when he was a child growing up in this country.

From Bombay Paul caught a train headed in a southeasterly direction across the Indian subcontinent to Madras, where he wandered around with his senses on overload: every smell, every scene, every sound drew his attention. He could hardly wait until Margaret arrived to experience this place he remembered so vividly.

Paul made another interesting discovery. Madras was located in the Tamil-speaking region of southern India. As he walked the streets of the city, Paul remembered some of the Tamil language he had easily spoken as a boy. Even though he had barely spoken a word of the language in twenty-three years, he could understand much of what people were saying. He could make himself partially understood in Tamil, though he realized there was a lot he had forgotten and would need to relearn.

After Paul had spent several days at a missionary guesthouse in Madras, James MacGilvray, a staff member from the hospital in Vellore, picked him up and drove him ninety miles west to Vellore. As they drove through the lush, emerald-green countryside, Paul peppered James with questions about his new home. He learned that the town of Vellore had a population of about three hundred thousand residents and that the Christian Medical College and Hospital was located in the heart of the city. James also told Paul a little about the history of the hospital and college. Ida Scudder, an American doctor who, like Paul, had been born of missionary parents in India, founded the place in 1900. Dr. Scudder had established the medical facility to both treat Indian women and train talented women as doctors. Over the years, the institution had grown in size and reputation and had now begun accepting male medical students. In fact, James pointed out, it was December 9, 1946, Ida Scudder's seventy-sixth birthday, and a celebration party was going on back at the college.

Upon arrival at Vellore, Paul unloaded his belongings outside the home of an American couple, Jack and Naomi Carman. Jack was head surgeon at the hospital, and he and his wife had the task of welcoming new doctors and helping them adjust to life in India.

The next day Paul set to work. He was amazed at the number of people who streamed through the hospital gates seeking medical attention. What was even more amazing than the numbers of people was their diversity. Paul saw men in business suits standing in line alongside beggars in loincloths, well-groomed women in immaculate saris, and women from the countryside clad in little more than rags. Children were everywhere. It was quite a sight to behold and, Paul realized, a tribute to the vision of Dr. Ida Scudder in founding an institution that ministered to the medical needs of the diverse Indian population.

Paul noticed one man amid the crowd waiting to be seen by hospital staff. The man waited patiently in line holding up his left arm and hand as if he were a policeman stopping traffic. When Paul inquired as to who the man was and why he was holding up his arm and hand, the man explained that he was a fakir, or holy man, and that fifteen years before he had made a religious vow never to lower his arm again and use it. As a result, his joints had fused and his muscles had atrophied. A nurse explained that the man was at the hospital not because of his fused arm but to seek treatment for a peptic ulcer. Paul walked away wondering how anyone could believe that his god would want him to give up the use of his arm and hand.

Jack Carman was not only the head surgeon at the hospital but also the only surgeon, and he was very glad when Paul arrived. It was decided that Paul would specialize in orthopedic surgery at Vellore, since he'd had some experience back in London.

Paul was kept busy in the operating theater attended by a contingent of nurses and assistants. Some of the operations he performed could take up to twelve hours, and by the time he was finished, his clothes were completely saturated with perspiration. Neither the hospital nor the operating theaters were air-conditioned, and in the hot season the temperature in Vellore could soar to 110 degrees Fahrenheit and beyond. Even though ceiling fans were fitted to the operating theaters, Paul would not allow them to be used while he operated for fear that they might blow contaminated dust and other particles into the incision. Despite the oppressive heat, Paul was eager to perform surgeries.

Paul also kept busy teaching a class at the medical college on surgical techniques. And then there was the blood bank. The hospital at Vellore was growing and preparing to undertake more advanced types of surgery. Part of this involved developing a blood bank with a ready supply of blood on hand. Paul threw his energy into this effort. From his time saving lives in hospitals in London during the war, he knew how important blood transfusions were. Paul helped to devise procedures to sterilize the blood after it was collected to ensure that it did not contain dangerous pathogens, such as bacteria and the hepatitis virus.

All this was easy. The challenge for Paul and the other doctors was getting Indians to donate blood. In Indian culture, blood was considered as important as one's life, and no one in his right mind would give away his lifeblood to save another life, even if that person was his child or spouse. The situation frustrated the doctors. A doctor would explain the need for life-saving blood to be donated by a relative of someone who needed surgery, and invariably the relatives would refuse. On one occasion Dr. Reeves Betts, a new arrival at Vellore from Boston, got so frustrated by the refusal of relatives of a girl needing emergency chest surgery that he rolled up his sleeve and called for Paul to drain off some of his own blood.

Paul immediately sized up Dr. Bett's ploy and played right into it, putting a cuff on the doctor's upper arm, inserting a needle into his vein, and then draining his blood into a bottle. Paul had collected a half pint of blood before two of the girl's uncles stepped forward and offered to donate. Paul quickly collected two pints of blood, and Reeves got to work operating on the young girl.

The ploy had worked, but Paul knew that Dr. Betts or any other doctor in the hospital couldn't keep giving a half pint of his or her blood to shame relatives into donating theirs. He came to realize that practicing medicine in India offered great opportunity to save lives and reduce people's levels of pain and suffering, but it was not without its challenges.

Paul had been at Vellore only a few days when he took off his shoes and threw them into the closet. From now on he was going to go barefoot or wear sandals. He had done so as a boy, and now as a grown man in India, he would do the same.

As the weeks flew by at the Christian Medical College and Hospital, Paul hardly noticed the turmoil that had engulfed the northern regions of India. The country was on the verge of civil war in the north as Indians pushed for independence from Great Britain. Hindus and Muslims clashed over having their own independent nations, and protests and riots took place in northern cities, such as Calcutta and Delhi, where hundreds of Hindus and Muslims were killed. It was a bitter dispute that almost went unnoticed in the south, where things remained calm and peaceful.

In fact, the only time Paul really thought about India's problems was when he'd get a letter from

Margaret. Between stories of the children, Margaret asked questions about the wisdom and safety of their all joining him in India. Paul found this confusing, and he wrote back explaining that Vellore was one of the most wonderful, peaceful places on earth and was just where God wanted them to be. Apparently his assurances were not enough for Margaret, because in late May, just two weeks before she and the children were due to sail from England, Paul received an odd telegram: "Is it really safe for us to come now? Margaret."

Puzzled by the telegram, Paul set out to get to the bottom of the situation. That was when he became aware of the volatile, civil war–like situation that existed in the north. When he read some of the headlines reported in the newspapers back in England, he understood his wife's concerns. He felt crushed. Why hadn't he taken the questions in Margaret's letters more seriously? Now it was too late. Given the political situation that existed, Paul did not have the heart to insist that his wife come to India when all she had been reading about the country for weeks back in England had been negative. He decided that it would make more sense for him to finish out the year at Vellore and return to England and discuss the situation in person with Margaret. Reluctantly he sent her a telegram: "Better you don't come now. I will return in March."

With a heavy heart that he would not be seeing his wife and children for at least another six months, Paul returned to work, trying to banish thoughts of how happy he would have been to have had Margaret at his side once again. He waited for a letter from his wife, but one did not come. Then, to his surprise, Paul was handed another telegram on June 15, 1947. He hardly dared to open it. Had something happened to one of the children? He unfolded the page and read. "Onboard the *Strathmore*. Arriving Bombay as planned. Margaret."

Paul let out a whoop of joy as he read the words. Margaret was coming after all! The telegram had been sent from Port Said, Egypt. Margaret was already on her way.

That afternoon Paul asked for time off to travel to Bombay to meet his family. Once in Bombay he bounded up the gangway and onto the *Strathmore*, eager to see his family once again. Now Paul could introduce them to the country he loved so much.

Chapter 9

A Fog Lifted

On board the *Strathmore* Paul engulfed Margaret in a huge hug and stood back to survey the children. "What's this?" he teased. "A band of refugees?"

Paul had to admit that they did look like a dejected group. Christopher and Jean were covered with heat rash and boils, and Margaret looked exhausted, with dark circles under her eyes. Paul reached out to hold Jean, who, not recognizing him, wailed and clung to her mother.

Margaret explained that it had been a hot and arduous journey from England. The children had been sick, and Margaret was looking forward to getting to Vellore to rest.

Vellore was a grueling two-and-a-half-day train trip away. Paul was grateful that his cousin Monica

Harris had been traveling on the same ship and had been able to assist Margaret with the children throughout the voyage. Monica was returning to her mission station in southern India and would be traveling with the Brands for the first two days of the journey. Paul hoped that she would assist him with the children on the journey and give Margaret some time to relax.

The train trip was every bit as arduous for his wife and children as Paul thought it would be. He noticed that Margaret found it difficult to deal with the Indians who swarmed around wanting to touch Christopher and Jean. Paul knew that those reaching out to squeeze the cheeks of his children meant well, but he was glad when Monica instructed them in perfect Tamil to stand back and give the family some room. As if people swarming around them was not enough, the hot season had begun and the furnace-like wind that blew into the window of the carriage made the ride almost unbearable.

At noon on June 29, 1947, the Brand family arrived in Vellore. They moved in with Jack and Naomi Carman until Margaret and the children could get acclimated to India and they could move into a place of their own. Soon, however, Paul could see that Margaret was still exhausted and having a hard time adjusting to the stifling heat of Vellore. He decided to take action.

"We must get you away to the hills," Paul said to Margaret as he scooped up three-year-old Christopher in his arms. "It will be cooler there, and we can all get used to being a family again." He could see the glimmer of relief in his wife's eyes.

Paul arranged to go up to the hill country station of Kotagiri in the Nilgiri Hills, where it was much cooler than on the plains and where most European mothers and their children spent the worst of the hot season.

Although Margaret wanted to do what she could to help the hospital at Vellore, she had not signed on as a doctor. As the spouse of a doctor, she was free to spend time settling the children into their newly adopted country.

The Brands loaded themselves onto a train for an overnight trip west to the foothills of the mountains of southern India. Once there, they boarded a bus for the drive up into the mountains to Kotagiri. Upon their arrival they moved into a small bungalow owned by the Kotagiri Medical Fellowship. When they were settled, Paul's mother, Granny Brand, visited them. Paul was struck by how much energy his mother still had as she spoke of the joy she found in assisting in the mobile eye clinics in Madras.

After a week at Kotagiri, Paul realized that Margaret and the children were not yet rested enough to endure the humid, rainy, hot season on the plains. He arranged for them to stay longer in Kotagiri while he returned to his duties at the hospital in Vellore. They could stay on in the bungalow if Margaret would help out at the Kotagiri Medical Fellowship, which consisted of a small hospital, a dispensary, and village clinics.

The situation was not ideal, but Paul felt much better knowing that his wife and children were only a two days' journey away instead of half a world away.

He had been living and working at Vellore for over six months and felt very much a part of the place. He could hardly wait until Margaret and the children were rested enough to join him in Vellore and they could move into their own place. In their four years of marriage, he and Margaret had not lived together as a unit.

On August 14, 1947, several weeks after Paul arrived back at Vellore from Kotagiri, news came that the British government had announced the partitioning of British India along religious lines into two separate nations. East and West Pakistan would be Muslim, and India would be Hindu. Paul hoped that this would bring an end to the political turmoil in the country, but instead it led to more violent clashes between Muslims and Hindus. Even so, with the two countries now established and independent, Paul thought it would be a matter of time before things worked themselves out. Besides, most of the violence and civil unrest in the nation seemed to bypass Vellore and much of South India.

At the hospital, Paul opened a foot clinic and was astounded when overnight it became the busiest clinic. The majority of the cases he saw at the clinic were clubfoot, a condition with which Paul had some experience. Paul had worked at Great Ormond Street Hospital in London with Dr. Denis Browne, a world expert in surgically correcting clubfoot in babies. Paul had noticed during his time at Great Ormond Street Hospital that such surgery created a lot of scar tissue, which in turn became a problem as the child grew. Nonetheless, surgically correcting clubfoot was the accepted procedure, and Paul decided to use it, despite its drawbacks.

Many of the patients coming to the clinic were clubfooted adults. Paul had never seen this in England, since clubfoot was corrected in infancy. It was disconcerting for Paul to see an adult walking on the side or top of his or her curled-under foot.

As he examined a young man of nineteen with clubfoot, Paul was amazed at how supple the man's foot tissue was. The foot had none of the hard scar tissue that came from surgical correction. Paul decided to try a different approach in treating the young man. He bent the foot around until the young man felt pain, at which point he set the foot in a cast. After a week he removed the cast and repeated the procedure of bending the foot until it hurt and putting it back in a cast. Over the next several weeks, as the procedure was repeated, Paul was able to restore the young man's foot to a normal position.

Paul was nearly as surprised as the young man at the outcome of the treatment. Soon this became the accepted procedure for treating clubfoot at the hospital. Instead of radical surgery to correct the deformity in one hit, Paul used a gradual approach that produced the same result with no later problems.

One day, during the steamy hot season, Dr. Cochrane sought Paul out. "How about coming over to Chingleput and having lunch with me?" he asked.

"I'd like that," Paul replied, thinking that it would be good to talk with Dr. Cochrane about the possibility of his staying long-term at the hospital in Vellore. As it would turn out, the two men ended up having quite a different conversation.

Later that week Paul was able to find the time to make the seventy-five-mile trip east to Chingleput, where Dr. Cochrane, the head of the medical school at Vellore, was the superintendent of the Lady Willingdon Leprosy Sanatorium. As he entered the gates of the sanatorium, Paul glanced at his watch. He had made good time from the train station and was a little early. Dr. Cochrane greeted him warmly and said, "Let's go for a walk before lunch. You've been in India for a while now, but since you're not assigned to any of the mobile clinics, I don't suppose you've seen many cases of leprosy."

Paul nodded. It was true. He had hardly seen or thought about leprosy since arriving at Vellore. He knew a little about the skin disease—that it was caused by the same bacteria seen in tuberculosis, that about 95 percent of people were naturally immune and could not catch the disease, and that those who did catch it were completely cut off from their previous world. This was true even in the hospital at Vellore, where lepers were left untreated for fear that treatment would cause rioting in the wards. That was about all Paul knew or felt he needed to know about the disease. After all, he was now an orthopedic surgeon, interested in bones, not skin.

Soon Paul was walking around the thousand-patient facility at Chingleput, admiring the way the staff worked with the patients. Dr. Cochrane told him that patients had been trained to give injections to each other, grow their own food, weave cloth for clothing and bandages, and even bind their own books.

"I like the way things are set up here," Paul commented. "It's well thought out and gives the lepers dignity. I have to admit, it's not at all like I imagined a leprous asylum to be."

"It's a hospital, not an asylum," Dr. Cochrane snapped. "And don't call them lepers. What comes to mind when you say the word *leper*?"

Paul's mind flashed back to when he was seven years old living in the Kolli Hills and the three lepers had come to the house seeking help. He recalled how his father had worn gloves, how his mother had burned the basket they touched, and how he and Connie had been warned never to go near the spot where the lepers had stood.

Apparently Dr. Cochrane was not expecting an answer to his question, because he continued, "Whatever it is you thought of, that's the stigma these people have to live with every day. They're not defiled or unclean, they have a disease—just like any other disease."

Paul nodded and mumbled an apology. He had hit a nerve with Dr. Cochrane. He reminded himself not to use the words *leper* or *asylum* again.

The two men continued their tour and were soon standing in a courtyard where many patients were sitting. Some of the people were blind, many had bandages on their hands and feet, and the chins and noses of some looked like they had been eaten away.

"Look at the skin nodule on this leg," Dr. Cochrane said, pointing to one patient, "and the discoloration of the skin around the cheeks," he added, pointing to another.

Paul felt depressed, especially when he thought about how these people would never get better. Their best hope was that a new class of sulfone drugs would slow the progress of their disease.

Paul's stomach growled, and he hoped the tour would soon be over. While he appreciated that Dr. Cochrane was a world expert on leprosy, skin diseases had never interested Paul. Besides, it was time for lunch. Suddenly, however, it was as if a fog had lifted and Paul was seeing the scene in front of him from an entirely different point of view. It almost made him gasp. He was no longer looking at pitiful people with an incurable skin disease. He was looking at people with hands—horribly deformed hands. Some of the hands looked like mittens, with all of the fingers gone, while other hands were set in a claw position or were raw and ulcerated. Never before had Paul seen so many people in one place with hand problems.

"I'm not interested in skin," Paul said to Dr. Cochrane. "I operate on hands. Tell me about these hands I'm seeing. What is wrong with them? How did they get that way? How are you treating them?"

Dr. Cochrane turned to Paul with a strange look on his face. "I'm sorry, Paul," he said. "I can't answer any of those questions."

"Why?"

"Because I don't know."

Paul studied the doctor's face. Was he joking? Dr. Robert Cochrane was a world-renowned expert on leprosy, and here in front of him were hundreds of lepers, most of whom had some kind of deformity in their hands—and their feet, for that matter—and the doctor did not seem to know anything about it!

"What do you mean you don't know? Isn't it your job to know?" Paul asked.

"My job?" Dr. Cochrane challenged. "My job? Paul, I am doing all I can. I am a skin man. I study their skin. It would take a bone man, an orthopedic surgeon, to figure out what is happening to their hands and feet. You're one of those. Tell me, is it your fault or mine that we don't yet know what's going on?"

"Surely someone has done studies, if not here, then somewhere. There must be papers in medical journals on such things as the deformed hands of leprosy sufferers," Paul exclaimed.

Dr. Cochrane shook his head sadly. "There are at least ten million leprosy patients in the world, and most of them have deformed hands. If this were any other disease, of course that would be the case—it would have been the object of multiple studies. But as I said, this is leprosy, and people, even doctors, recoil when they see it."

Paul felt himself turning red. Had Dr. Cochrane seen the fear on his face when he recalled the three lepers from his childhood? "But still," Paul went on, unable to believe his fellow doctor, "someone, somewhere must have looked at the problem."

Dr. Cochrane again shook his head, and the two men walked in silence. As they walked, Paul noticed directly in front of them a teenage boy struggling to unbuckle his sandals with clawlike hands. Paul stopped.

"Nerve damage," Dr. Cochrane said. "That's about all I can tell you. Nerve damage, paralysis, and complete anesthesia."

"You mean he can't feel anything with his hands?" Paul asked.

"That's right. Numbing of the skin is one of the classic signs of leprosy. You could stick a pin into that hand and he wouldn't flinch. Some of them do it, a kind of grotesque party trick, if you will."

Paul drew in a deep breath and bent down. It was time to take a closer look. "May I see your hands?" he asked in Tamil.

"Yes," the teenager replied as he scrambled to his feet.

Paul took the boy's right hand. It was the first time he had ever touched a leprosy patient. He stroked the palm and then the fingers, which were stiff and inflexible. "Can you feel this?" he asked as he pressed down hard on one of the young man's knuckles.

"No," the teenager replied.

"Or this?" Paul said, choosing a different part of the boy's hand on which to apply pressure.

"No, I can't feel anything with my hands."

A wave of incredible sadness washed over Paul. This young man could not feel anything in his hands. It was as if his hands were lumps of meat at the end of his arms. And at least ten million other people in the world were suffering in the same way. It seemed impossible that Paul had not noticed it before.

Suddenly Paul realized that not all of the muscles could be paralyzed. Hadn't the boy been able to grasp the sandal strap? Paul put his hand into the boy's palm once again. "Squeeze my hand as hard as you can," he instructed.

A jolt of intense pain shot up Paul's arm. The boy had a vice-like grip, as strong as any person's grip. Paul felt a surge of hope. The hand had working muscles! Strong muscles.

Paul thanked the boy and moved on, peppering Dr. Cochrane with questions: At what stage of the disease did the fingers fall off? Did the doctor have any unattached fingers Paul could study? Had Dr. Cochrane noticed any patterns in numbing on the skin? Did all leprosy patients get ulcers and sores, and what caused them? Had anyone operated on clawed hands or traced the nerves to see which ones might be responsible for the lack of feeling?

Dr. Cochrane did not have any answers to Paul's questions and kept insisting that no one else did either. Paul found this impossible to believe.

Even as Paul ate vegetable curry for lunch and chatted more with Dr. Cochrane, his mind was moving a million miles an hour. There had to be answers in the hospital research library back in Vellore, and he was going to find them.

New Hope

Paul worked ten hours a day operating on patients and teaching medical students, and he was on call every third night, but now he had another mission. He spent every spare moment in the hospital library running down all the leads he could find on leprosy. His drive to know more was infectious. Soon other doctors at the hospital were giving up their own off-hours to cover for Paul so that he could continue his research in the library.

After three months Paul had to conclude that Dr. Cochrane had been right: no one had studied the deterioration of the hands or feet of leprosy patients. The only references Paul could find in all of the medical journals were related to how to amputate the arms and legs of a leprosy sufferer once the limbs had become too infected and ulcerated. Thousands of orthopedic surgeons around the world operated regularly on patients with hand problems caused by polio, birth defects, and accidents, but not one of them had ever operated on the hands of a leprosy patient. Paul found this hard to comprehend, since there were more leprosy patients with hand problems than all of the other patients with hand problems combined.

Like an annoying stone in his shoe, Paul could not ignore the mystery of leprosy. Somebody had to solve the riddle of what was happening to the hands of leprosy sufferers and why. Eventually Paul came to the conclusion that this was the reason God had put him at Vellore—to be the person who took on the task of helping leprosy patients keep or regain the use of their hands.

By now it was October, the end of the hot season on the plains, and time for Margaret to move down to Vellore. It was a wonderful day for Paul when he was able to escort his wife and children down from the mountains and back to Vellore. The family would continue staying with the Carmans while Margaret adjusted to living in Vellore and managing a household in India, and then they would move into a place of their own.

Paul could not have been happier. For the first time the Brand family was living in one place. It made coming home from work after a long day a joy. In the evenings he could relax and sit and talk with

Margaret. One of the things he talked with her about was his determination to find out more about the way leprosy affected people's hands. Margaret was very supportive of his efforts, and Paul was glad he had married a fellow doctor who could understand his passion for this medical mystery.

It was good that Margaret supported him in his quest, because Paul spent many of his off-hours studying the problem. He decided that the best way to proceed would be to study a small group of leprosy patients and possibly operate on their hands. Vellore seemed the perfect spot to do this, since it was right in the middle of the highest density of leprosy in the world. Three out of every one hundred people in the Madras area were afflicted with the disease.

Paul asked Dr. Norman Macpherson, the medical superintendent of the hospital, whether he could have a few beds for leprosy patients. The conversation did not go well. Dr. Macpherson was kind but firm in his response: No leprosy patients had been or would be allowed in the hospital. Chingleput, not a "regular" hospital like the one in Vellore, was the place for leprosy patients. Leprosy patients simply did not belong in the general hospital population, because that would cause fear, even panic, among the other patients and staff. Paul found Dr. Macpherson's second reason the most maddening: leprosy patients, he said, had "bad flesh" and it was pointless to operate on a patient who would not recover properly. Such thinking infuriated Paul. The reason there was no hope for leprosy patients was that they were always isolated in colonies and had no access to the specialists who might be able to help them.

Paul did not let Dr. Macpherson's rejection of his plan stop his quest. If the leprosy patients could not come to him, he would go to them. He talked the situation over with Margaret, who agreed that he should go to the Lady Willingdon Leprosy Sanatorium in Chingleput each weekend to begin a scientific survey of the patients there. Paul spoke so enthusiastically about the idea that several others at Vellore pledged to help him in any way they could. Dr. Ida Scudder, namesake and niece of the hospital's founder, was the head of the radiology department, and she put her staff and facilities at Paul's disposal. Members of the pathology and dermatology departments also offered to do what they could.

But where to start? Paul knew his first task was to survey the patients at Chingleput to determine the type of condition of each person's hands. He repeatedly examined the hands of every leprosy patient available, testing the patient's sensation, first with a pin, then with a feather. He measured the movement of each person's fingers and thumbs and determined which muscles were paralyzed, which nerves had thickened, and which fingers were missing.

As the weeks passed, Paul became excited with his results. It was obvious to him that the paralysis caused by leprosy followed a distinct, uniform pattern. Some patients with the disease might progress through the stages on the way to paralysis faster than others, but all leprosy patients went through the same stages. Soon Paul knew which muscles the disease would paralyze and which muscles would be unaffected. Paul now knew that perfectly good muscles were in place that he could surgically manipulate to take over from the paralyzed ones. There was hope of giving leprosy patients back some limited use of their hands.

The next thing Paul had to do was find out whether the flesh of leprosy patients was really "bad"—meaning that the flesh of the leprosy sufferer was infected with the disease and therefore would never heal. What good was doing surgery if the incisions would never heal? Paul did not believe this was the case, but because he did not know for sure, he took many flesh samples from the hands of leprosy patients and sent them to the pathology laboratory at the hospital in Vellore for testing. The result from all the samples was the same: there was no disease in the tissue, and under the microscope the sample appeared normal except for a smaller number of blood vessels and the absence of nerve endings. As far as the pathology reports were concerned, leprosy patients had "good" flesh, not "bad" flesh—flesh that could be coaxed to heal after an operation.

The one thing Paul had not yet discovered was what happened to the fingers of leprosy sufferers. How did they fall off? And with so many missing fingers, why weren't fingers lying around like fallen leaves? Paul carefully drew outlines of patients' hands over time to compare what was happening to the fingers. Yes, often parts of a patient's finger or fingers would disappear, but more often than not the patients were unaware of the loss. And when this was pointed out to them, they had no idea of how, when, or where it had happened.

Paul was pleased with what he had learned, but he knew that he had a long way to go. The problem in helping leprosy patients recover some use of their hands was twofold. First was understanding the clawing aspect of the fingers. Paul was reasonably sure that given enough time he could figure out how to take good muscles in the hands and reassign them to finger movement, so that a muscle that had previously worked the little finger could bend the thumb. The second issue was helping patients understand what was happening to their fingers and how to prevent finger loss. This would happen not with a surgeon's scalpel but by continuing the thousands of tiny measurements and observations that Paul was making and recording each week. Paul knew that over time some kind of pattern would emerge. He just had to stick to the task long enough to find out what was happening.

At the beginning of 1948, Paul felt that he had done enough research on the first part of the problem to try surgery on the paralyzed hand of a leprosy patient. He approached Dr. Cochrane and asked him to refer one leprosy patient to him who had nothing to lose, someone whose hands had been completely destroyed by the disease. Soon Paul was face-to-face with a new patient—Krishnamurthy—a young

Hindu man who had recently arrived at the leprosy sanatorium at Chingleput.

"You can't possibly make him any worse," Dr. Cochrane had told Paul, who, as soon as he examined Krishnamurthy's hands, had to agree. The only muscle the young man had any control over was his thumb, and even that was weak. There was no way that he could pick up anything, dress himself, feed himself, or take care of his own toilet needs. His feet, Paul noted grimly, were in worse condition than his hands. They ran with open ulcers. Paul did not have to wonder what living with leprosy had done to the young man; he could see it clearly in his eyes, which were filled with despair and hopelessness.

As Paul questioned Krishnamurthy, the young man had no expectation that any operation would help him in the slightest. He just looked forward to being fed regularly and having somewhere soft to sleep. He did not see himself as a pioneer, nor did he derive any excitement at the thought of being the first leprosy patient in history to have his hands operated on. At first Paul thought Krishnamurthy might not be intelligent enough to grasp the potential significance of the operation. After talking with him several times, however, Paul had to revise his opinion.

Krishnamurthy was a very intelligent young man from a prominent family. He spoke several languages and had a good job—that is, until he discovered a blemish on his skin, which soon became numb. He knew immediately what it was, the worst curse of all. Within weeks he had lost his job, his family, and his home and was wandering through the streets like a beggar. This swift change had made Krishnamurthy despondent, and hunger had eventually overcome pride, bringing him to the gates of the Lady Willingdon Leprosy Sanatorium.

Although Paul was mostly interested in Krishnamurthy's hands, he decided that the man's twisted feet were a more urgent concern. As a result of the paralysis in his feet from leprosy, Krishnamurthy tended to walk on the outer edges. Paul wondered whether it was possible to perform tenodesis on his feet. Tenodesis had been used on some polio sufferers who developed a similar foot deformity as a result of their disease. Tenodesis required the moving of tendons and reattaching them to the bone in such a way that they would pull the foot straight. Paul decided to give it a try. Much to his delight, the operation was a complete success. Soon Krishnamurthy was walking on feet that were straight. The soles of his feet were landing squarely on the ground, avoiding the infected ulcers that had resulted from walking incorrectly.

With Krishnamurthy's feet correctly aligned and the ulcers healed, Paul decided it was time to do what he really wanted to do—operate on the young man's hands. Through his research, Paul understood why the hands of leprosy patients assumed a claw-like position. He had worked out which of the seventy muscles controlling the movement of the hands were responsible. The ulnar nerve was one of the nerves destroyed by the leprosy bacilli (bacteria), and since this nerve controlled the intrinsic muscles of the hand, its deterioration effectively paralyzed those muscles. As a result, the flexor muscles in the forearm, which did not become paralyzed, pulled on the fingers and caused them to bend toward the palm of the hand in a clawlike way.

With this knowledge Paul decided to try a surgical technique known as Bunnell's operation, which had been developed during World War I to correct hand disabilities from war injuries. Like the foot surgery, this operation had been employed to help polio patients regain use of their hands. The procedure involved repurposing the flexor sublimis digitorum muscles that controlled the bending of the second joint of the fingers to take over for the paralyzed intrinsic muscles.

Paul and his surgical assistant went to work on the delicate operation that involved detaching the muscles, splitting the tendons in two, rethreading the tendons through the palm of the hand, and reattaching the tendons to the top of the fingers.

During the first surgery, Paul performed Bunnell's operation on only two of Krishnamurthy's fingers. In a subsequent surgery he repeated the operation on all of his fingers. Of course, a lot of physical therapy followed, as the flexor sublimis digitorum muscles had to be trained to work the fingers differently from how they had been intended to work. In the end the operation was a success, and Krishnamurthy regained some use of his paralyzed hands.

Even though Paul tried to downplay the operation he had carried out on Krishnamurthy, word began to spread that something astonishing had happened. Words like *breakthrough* and *new hope* were being bandied about. Even though Paul was happy with the outcome of the surgeries, he cautioned people that many more steps had to be taken before they could reach any definitive conclusions about the effectiveness of the procedure.

Paul was delighted when he learned that Krishnamurthy had reached a conclusion of his own. Once he regained some use of his hands, he was again able to feed himself and hold a book. It was as if he had awakened from a bad dream. He asked questions and joked with the staff. But most of all, Krishnamurthy wanted to know what motivated Paul and the nursing staff who now tended him to work with such diligence and compassion. Person after person explained to the young Hindu man that they were following the teachings of Jesus. Eventually Krishnamurthy decided that he, too, wanted to follow Jesus. Paul attended the young man's baptism, where he chose the new name of John.

In the weeks that followed, Paul watched as John studied the Bible, holding it solidly in his hands. Paul felt a deep sense of satisfaction in serving the bodies and souls of the Indian people. Perhaps one day he would make some medical breakthroughs that would serve leprosy patients all over the world.

For now, Paul had another obstacle to overcome. He knew that he had to understand more about the nerves of people with leprosy. The only way to do this was to extract some nerve tissue and view it under a microscope. In order to accomplish this, he needed to perform autopsies on the dead bodies of leprosy patients. This created a problem. Muslim mullahs (scholars) decreed that it was unholy to cut into a body after death, and the Hindu religion required that the entire body be burned upon a person's death. Strict Hindus would not even allow an arm or a leg with gangrene to be amputated, even if they knew the person would die without amputation.

To overcome this obstacle, other departments at the hospital in Vellore used the bodies of dead prisoners or of those with no family ties on which to perform scientific autopsies, but very few of these people had leprosy. Paul put the word out as far away as Bombay and Hyderabad: "Telephone or telegraph me any time of the day or night if a leprosy patient dies and you have permission to do an autopsy." He also instructed his assistant, Ceylonese Dr. Gusta Buultgens, to prepare the sample jars filled with formalin and the surgical instruments necessary to perform an autopsy. Then he prayed for a phone call.

Chapter 11

A Body Reveals Its Secrets

Family life for the Brands continued. With the arrival of the hot season in 1948, Margaret and the children once again retreated to the mountains in Kotagiri. Margaret was pregnant and expecting another baby in October 1948 and was glad to be away from the sweltering heat of the plains.

While his family was gone, Paul moved into a new duplex on the medical college campus. College Hill, as the campus was called, was located four miles from the hospital on the edge of Vellore.

In September, at the end of the hot season, Margaret and the children arrived back in Vellore and moved into the duplex with Paul. On October 22, 1948, Margaret gave birth to a daughter, whom they named Mary. As Paul welcomed Mary into the world, he thought about how different the circumstances were from Christopher's birth back in London: no bombs, no fires, and no ration cards.

One evening, two weeks after Mary was born, a messenger arrived at the door with a note for Margaret. Paul heard her groan as she read it.

"Listen to this," Margaret said. "It's from Dr. Carol Jameson. 'I don't want to hurry you, but we are very short at Schell, and we would be glad if you would pop in there for a few hours each day and just keep an eye on things.'"

"I'm sorry," Paul said. He knew that his wife had offered to help out in any of the medical departments at the hospital except the Schell Eye Hospital.

"I really don't know a thing about eyes," Margaret lamented. "I missed that rotation in medical school because of the bombings. It would take me years to learn. I'd be much better in pediatrics."

Margaret then sent a note back to Carol apologizing for not knowing anything about eyes and thus being the wrong choice for the job. Both Paul and Margaret assumed that the decline would be the end of it, but an hour later the messenger returned. This time the note from Carol read, "You'll learn. Please start on Monday."

"It doesn't sound like you have much chance arguing with Carol," Paul said. "Perhaps you should try it and see how it goes."

"Do I have a choice?" Margaret sighed, shrugging her shoulders.

Paul felt for his wife. He knew how much she liked to master a subject, and he could see how deflated she

was about having to start out in a new area. Even the
nurses in the Schell Eye Hospital would know more
than she did.

A few weeks later, while Paul was enjoying a rare
moment of relaxation before dinner, the telephone
rang. Paul picked it up and heard the voice of Dr.
Harry Paul from the leprosarium in Chingleput. The
connection was noisy with static, but Paul could
understand what Harry was saying. An elderly male
leprosy patient had died at the leprosarium and
would be cremated in the morning. Paul and his team
could do what they wanted with the body, as long as
it was sewn up and in one piece by dawn tomorrow.

Paul had waited a long time for such a call, and
he dared not turn the opportunity down, although
it meant he had to work fast. He briefly explained
the situation to Margaret and ran out the door. All
thoughts of dinner evaporated. An hour later he was
driving a borrowed Land Rover on the road to Chingleput with a technician named Jayaraj beside him,
Dr. Gusta Buultgens in the back seat, hundreds of
tiny specimen jars filled with formalin neatly packed
into boxes, and the instruments they would need for
the autopsy.

Paul was nervous about the seventy-five-mile
drive from Vellore to Chingleput. Under normal
conditions this distance could be covered in less
than two hours, but nothing about driving in India
was normal. Motor vehicles shared potholed roads
with pedestrians, bicyclists, bullock carts, and cows.
Because cows were sacred in Hindu society, they
always had the right of way. During the day it was

easy to spot them on the road, but not so at night. Night driving required great concentration and constant vigilance for sharing the road.

It took every ounce of Paul's concentration to keep the vehicle moving forward at a modest rate. Paul glanced at his watch. It was already eleven o'clock, and they had only just passed through the town of Kancheepuram, the halfway mark on the journey. The town, with its towering temple turrets, looked very different in the moonlight.

As they drove on, Paul felt a sudden intense heat on his feet. He looked down and saw flames shooting up through the opening in the vehicle's floor and engulfing his sandaled feet. Paul pulled his feet away from the pedals as fast as he could and swerved to the side of the road. Because of the flames, he could no longer use the brake pedal. He yelled for his passengers to brace themselves as he steered toward a clump of shrubs at the side of the road. The Land Rover crashed into the shrub, which slowed its momentum.

As the vehicle lurched to a stop, everyone jumped out. Paul pulled branches from a nearby shrub to beat out the flames. He was grateful to see Dr. Buultgens grabbing the specimen jars and instruments from the back of the vehicle. Meanwhile, Jayaraj scooped up sand to help Paul extinguish the fire. Everyone worked fast before the flames could reach the gas tank.

Within a few minutes the fire had died out. Paul wrapped his hand in a rag and gingerly opened the hood. Smoke billowed out, and as it thinned, Paul could make out a mass of melted wires in the glow of a flashlight beam. "This Land Rover won't be going anywhere soon," he said. "We'd better start walking."

Leaving the Land Rover at the side of the road, Paul and his two helpers hoisted the boxes of specimen jars and instruments onto their shoulders and started walking. Paul hoped that someone would come along and pick them up, but as they trudged on, his hope faded. Not a single car or bus passed them. The only vehicles on the road were bullock carts, passing like shadows in the night, headed in the opposite direction. The trio walked on, keeping a weary eye to the east. Paul wondered whether they would still be walking when dawn broke.

Paul's mood brightened when he realized that the next town was home to a Christian mission school. Perhaps they would find someone at the school who could drive them the rest of the way to Chingleput. A short time later they reached the school and roused the teacher from his bed. The teacher did not have a car, but he offered them all a bed for the remainder of the night. Paul had not come this far to give up, and he persuaded the teacher to get dressed and go in search of a car they could hire. This was a tall order. It was after midnight, but the teacher eventually returned with a car and driver.

Soon Paul and his assistants were again headed for Chingleput, and at two-thirty in the morning, the weary medical team pulled up to the gate of the leprosarium. Everything was dark and quiet. Paul banged on the gate, and a watchman carrying a kerosene hurricane lamp shuffled over to see what the commotion was.

Paul identified himself and explained that Dr. Paul had given him permission to enter the grounds and perform an autopsy. The night watchman recoiled at the word and held up his hands to indicate he wanted nothing to do with the conversation. Paul took a deep breath, aware that it was going to take all his skills of diplomacy to get through the gate. The old man lay between him and the body Paul so desperately needed to examine.

Paul was adamant with the night watchman that he was not about to turn around and leave, especially after all he had been through to get this far. Eventually the watchman relented and told the group to follow him. Leaving the driver in the car at the gate, Paul, Dr. Buultgens, and Jayaraj, their instruments and specimen jars in tow, made their way behind some huts and followed a winding, rocky, uphill trail. After about ten minutes of walking, the watchman stopped in front of a tiny stucco hut and opened the door. The smell of a corpse in the Indian heat hit Paul immediately. The watchman shrugged as if to tell them he thought they were crazy to go inside, and then handed over his kerosene lamp and disappeared. The hut had no electricity, and Paul was very grateful for the lamp, which hung from the central beam of the roof.

The hut was empty except for a long wooden table, on top of which lay the body of an elderly man. Paul surveyed the body while the other two unpacked the specimen jars and laid out the instruments. The man had severely deformed hands, almost no fingers and toes, and a reduced nose. He was a perfect example of what the ravages of leprosy could do to one's body.

Paul glanced at his watch. It was three o'clock. In just three and a half hours the sun would come up, and they had much to do before then. They all donned rubber aprons and gloves, which made Paul start sweating in the stifling heat. With the efficiency of a surgical team and the aid of a small flashlight, the researchers set to work. Paul began on one side of the cadaver to make long cuts the length of the arm and leg. He rolled back skin, fat, and muscle tissue to expose the nerves.

Meanwhile, Dr. Buultgens started work on the other side of the cadaver. She took nerve samples every two inches up and down the leg and arm. Jayaraj placed each sample in a formalin-filled specimen jar and wrote a detailed label for each jar. These nerve specimens would be studied later under the laboratory microscope.

The group worked quickly and mostly in silence, the only sound being the buzz of cicadas outside and the hiss of the kerosene lamp overhead. At the end of three hours Paul had made great progress. He had uncovered most of the cadaver's nerves from where they emerged from the spinal cord to the extremities.

He had also exposed the nerves of the face, seeking to discover the cause of both eyelid paralysis and nose reduction in leprosy patients.

By now Paul had not slept in twenty-four hours, and the muscles in his back were tight from being hunched over the cadaver. As Paul stopped to stretch and gently massage the muscles in his lower back, the early morning sun crept above the horizon. Beams of golden sunlight streamed into the hut, filling the room with light other than the dim glow of the kerosene lamp and the small flashlight, the batteries of which were starting to wear down. When Paul turned back to examine his work, he was amazed by what he saw. His eyes ran up and down the exposed nerves. "Look at the nerve swellings," he declared as Dr. Buultgens leaned over to observe.

Such swelling of the nerves was an abnormality and was clearly visible behind the ankle, above the knee, at the wrist, and just above the elbow. The same swelling was also visible on the facial nerves where they branched at the cheek and chin. Paul knew that the swelling was a result of the leprosy infection. But he had not expected to see it at only a few key sites where the particular nerve ran close to the surface of the skin, such as the ulnar nerve just above the elbow. The nerves that were embedded deeper in the tissue were not affected at all by the leprosy, and Paul recognized that this was why some muscles were paralyzed in a leprosy sufferer while other muscles were not. But he had no idea why the nerve swellings occurred where they did.

"Perhaps because they are close to the surface they are more susceptible to impact damage," Dr. Buultgens surmised.

Paul nodded. It was possible. Only time would tell if her hypothesis was right.

Paul studied the cadaver more closely, trying to get a better idea of which muscles could be repurposed surgically to take over for those that were paralyzed. He took a series of photographs of the exposed nerves. By then it was time to suture the body and take it to be cremated on a funeral pyre, as was the Hindu custom.

After gathering all the specimen jars and surgical instruments, a tired Paul and his two assistants headed for the gate of the leprosarium. They then woke up their driver and headed back to Vellore.

Back at the hospital at Vellore, Paul sent the nerve samples from the autopsy to the pathology department, where Dr. Gault and his staff set to work analyzing them under the microscope. The process was long and slow. Being a thorough researcher, Paul waited patiently for the conclusions.

Over the next few months, Paul and his team performed seven more autopsies on leprosy cadavers, though none was as harrowing as the first autopsy in Chingleput. In each case they found the same nerve swellings in the same places in the bodies they autopsied. This was evidence to Paul that he was on to a breakthrough in understanding the way leprosy affected nerves. Paul just didn't know how to interpret the evidence. Why did the nerves swell at the particular places they did? What could possibly be the cause?

Paul received permission to keep several amputated hands to study, which he stored in the family freezer at home. At night he would often thaw out a hand and begin pulling the muscles and tendons in various directions with various intensities, trying to work out which muscles and tendons controlled what movements and which ones he could substitute for others.

Margaret did not tell the family cook what the objects wrapped up in the freezer were for fear he would run away. Sometimes the cook would ask if he could use the meat wrapped in the freezer, but Margaret told him they were keeping it for something special. The children, on the other hand, knew what Paul was up to and were delighted to sit beside him at the table while he described to them and demonstrated the marvels of the human hand.

Although Paul was busy with his regular hospital rounds and surgeries, he kept focused on his quest to discover just how leprosy debilitated the bodies of those it ravaged. Sometimes he experienced setbacks that made him question whether he would ever make significant progress. One of these setbacks occurred with John (as Krishnamurthy now called himself) some time after he had been released from the hospital. The day John was released had been a great day of celebration for Paul and the team of nurses and physical therapists who had worked with him. After his release from the hospital, John had returned to his family, shown them his working hands, and looked for a job to support himself. Sadly, things did not go as he had hoped.

One day, about two months after he had been released from the hospital, John returned to Vellore looking thin and forlorn. He held out his hands to Paul. "Sahib doctor," he said, using a term of respect, "these are bad hands. They are not good hands."

Paul felt his heart racing. How could the operation have gone wrong after such a long time? "What do you mean?" he asked, noting the tears in John's eyes.

"Bad begging hands, Sahib. Before, when I would beg, people would throw me money, but now they look at me and think I could work. But I cannot. No one will give me a job. People do not pity me, but they will not employ me either. It is because of my bad hands."

Paul was aghast. Why hadn't he thought about this before now? He recalled seeing another leprosy patient unbandaging himself and picking at his wounds, making it impossible for his hands to heal. Had that patient been worried about "bad begging hands" as well?

John interrupted his thoughts. "What should I do?"

The question hung in the air. What should he do? Paul did not have an answer, but he realized that unless he came up with one soon, all of his research would be pointless. If leprosy patients did not want to be healed because it gave them bad begging hands, then he might as well stop now.

As he thought about the dilemma, Paul decided that what was needed was a place where leprosy patients could earn a living right in Vellore. In an instant he could see it all: a small village with huts where those who had undergone surgery on their hands could live while they recovered. Physical therapists could observe the movements of their hands and guide them toward a trade suited to the kind of movement they had. Skilled instructors would train them in that trade. When they reached proficiency, the patients could return to their village and set up a small business.

It all seemed so simple and straightforward, and Paul wondered why he hadn't thought of it sooner. There was just one problem: it was difficult enough paying for the limited amount of research he was doing, and Paul wondered where the money for such a rehabilitation center would come from.

Chapter 12

Nava Jeeva Nilayam

A few days after coming up with the idea of a leprosy rehabilitation village, Paul was making his hospital rounds when one of his patients called him over. Mother Eaton, as the woman was affectionately known, was an eighty-four-year-old American missionary suffering from rheumatoid arthritis. She had come to Vellore hoping to get some relief from her pain, but there was little that could be done for her. Mother Eaton did not let the excruciating pain stop her from taking an active interest in what was happening at the hospital.

"Do you remember how yesterday you were telling me about your idea for a village for your leprosy patients?" she asked Paul.

"Yes," he replied.

"I couldn't sleep last night because of the pain, and I lay awake thinking about what a wonderful difference your idea could make in those boys' lives. I'm not a rich woman. I have only about five hundred pounds in the bank, but I kept thinking, how would I explain to my Lord why I left that money idle? I want you to take it and use it."

Paul felt tears fill his eyes. "Are you sure?" he asked.

Mother Eaton waved her hand. "Yes! I don't have long to live; we both know that. I want the money to go to build some small huts and a shed where those boys can learn a trade. In a year or two, they can go home and become self-sufficient, and other boys can come. What are you going to call the place?"

Paul took Mother Eaton's hands. "If you are sure this is what you want to do, we'll start right away. The need is great. I was thinking of calling it Nava Jeeva Nilayam."

"Perfect!" Mother Eaton responded enthusiastically. "New Life Center. I will pray for you every day."

Paul soon found out that he needed every one of Mother Eaton's prayers. Even those who Paul thought would enthusiastically support his plan were reticent. Among them was Dr. Cochrane, who pointed out to Paul that the new Schieffelin Leprosy Research Sanatorium was being planned for Vellore. Why not wait for it to be completed? Paul pointed out that he needed something now, and the site for the new research sanatorium had lain idle for over two years.

When Paul sought permission to build the rehabilitation village in the corner of the two-hundred-
acre lot on which the medical college stood, many
doctors at the hospital questioned such a move. They
argued that it was unwise to put medical students
and leprosy patients in such close proximity to each
other. Nonetheless, Paul persevered. He was granted
permission to build the village on the condition that
it be cordoned off with a barbed-wire fence and that
none of the inhabitants of the village cross the fence
and enter the medical college campus.

Paul accepted these conditions and set to work.
Soon he was busier than ever, designing and building
the New Life Center. He still had his hospital work to
do during the day and was regularly on call during
nights at the hospital. He also continued to spend his
weekends at Chingleput. And somewhere between
dusk and bedtime each night he pored over the plans
for the simple village. For the first time he marveled
at how his years as a builder were now helping him
with his work.

Meanwhile, the Brand family continued to grow.
On February 25, 1950, Margaret gave birth to a third
daughter, Estelle. Soon afterward the first group of six
young men were situated in the whitewashed, mud-
walled huts at the New Life Center. Because leprosy
did not respect social or caste boundaries, it was an
interesting group of men from both upper and lower
castes. Also, the men possessed a broad range of edu-
cational abilities. One of the residents was an engineer, another had a bachelor of science degree, and

still another had been a chartered accountant. Yet all of them had been afflicted with leprosy. And all of them living together in the village as they did was unique in India, a society deeply divided along caste and social lines.

At first Paul played the role of both doctor and instructor. Drawing on experience from his apprenticeship as a builder, he began teaching the young men how to work with wood—how to use the various tools to shape and mold the wood into beautiful and useful objects that could be sold for profit. The men started by making wooden toys and branched out from there. They also planted and tended a village garden where they learned to grow and cultivate a variety of vegetables to eat.

While the village was devoted to rehabilitation and teaching new trades to those who had regained the use of their hands through surgery, Paul had another reason for working so hard to make the New Life Center a reality. The village would provide him with a group of patients whom he could monitor and observe every day, unlike those patients at the leprosarium in Chingleput whom he saw only once a week.

By paying close attention to this small group, Paul hoped to unravel the mystery of why the fingers and toes of leprosy patients wasted away. As soon as the six men were settled in the New Life Center, he set out to find answers. With the help of Dr. Buultgens, now Paul's full-time research assistant, and several others, each patient's hands were inspected every evening, and any minute changes were recorded. That, however, was not the procedure that led to a major breakthrough.

The breakthrough came when one of the residents, a ten-year-old boy, offered to turn a key in a rusty lock for Paul. Paul was trying to unlock the padlock on a small storage room at the New Life Center, but the lock had rusted, and he could not manage to get the key to turn. That was when the ten-year-old boy came along and said, "Sahib doctor, let me try. I can do it."

The young boy grasped the key between his thumb and forefinger, and with a quick flick of his wrist, turned the key and undid the lock. "There, Sahib," the boy said with a grin, adding jokingly, "Are you a weakling?"

The boy's action was amazing to Paul, who had used all the force he could muster to turn that key until his fingers hurt. But this boy had done the seemingly impossible, turning the key in a lock that an adult could not turn. As he looked at the boy, Paul noticed several drops of blood falling to the floor. "Let me see your hand," he said.

As the boy held out his hand, Paul could see that in the process of turning the key he had applied so much pressure that he had cut his finger open to the bone. Yet because of the lack of feeling in his fingers, the boy was totally unaware of the damage he had done to himself.

Paul was amazed when he became aware that the men were probably damaging themselves in many ways every day without ever realizing it. It all made sense! When those wounds healed, they would leave behind scar tissue. And as that scar tissue built up over time under the skin, the blood vessels and fat tissue receded and created the shortening of the fingers that occurred in leprosy patients.

With this understanding, Paul began to spend his evenings and any spare time watching the men at the New Life Center work. Just as he thought, the men were constantly injuring their fingers without even noticing. Paul began to work with the men to make them more watchful for injuries. He redesigned many of the tools the men were using. He made sure that the tools had large, smooth handles with no sharp edges so that if they were gripped too hard, they would not cause lacerations of the fingers.

Paul taught the men to use pliers to hold the nails they were hammering so that they would not injure their fingers with the hammer. He also discovered that the blisters many of the men had on the sides of their hands were formed when the men turned off their kerosene lanterns at night—their hands inadvertently coming in contact with the lantern's hot glass. He had wooden extenders fitted to the control knobs of the lanterns so that the men's hands would stay a safe distance from the hot glass.

Paul still did not know whether the way some leprosy patients lost large sections of their fingers was part of the disease. Despite the great number of missing fingers, no one had ever managed to bring a lost finger to him so he could determine the reason for its having fallen off.

Then one morning at the New Life Center one of the young men showed his hand to Paul. Nearly a third of his index finger was missing. Paul asked him what had happened to it.

"Sahib doctor, I do not know," the young man replied. "My whole finger was there yesterday. Last night you even measured it."

"Where is the piece of your finger that is missing?" Paul asked.

The young man had no idea what had happened to his finger during the night. All he knew was that it was there when he went to bed and gone when he awoke.

Paul went to the young man's hut to investigate and see whether he could find the missing piece of finger. But he found no finger on or near the young man's sleeping mat. All he could see was drops of blood.

"Sahib doctor, look," one of the other men said who was helping Paul search.

Paul cast his eyes in the direction the man was pointing, and there he saw not the missing piece of the young man's finger but some more spots of blood and the trail of a rat's feet in the dust of the earthen floor of the hut. The young man's finger had not fallen off. A rat had gnawed it off in the night to feast on. Because the young man lacked feeling, he had not even been aware of it as he slept. Given the number of rats in India, Paul wondered how many other leprosy sufferers over the years had lost their fingers in the night.

The rat problem at the New Life Center was fixed by the introduction of cats to the complex. When any of the residents returned to their village to ply the trade they had learned at the rehabilitation village, they took a cat with them.

By now twelve men were living at the New Life Center. Knowing how susceptible their fingers were to injury, they all watched out for each other, checking up to make sure no one had inadvertently injured himself. Paul was pleased with this teamwork of patients helping patients. Not only did it speed the rehabilitation process, but also it gave each person a greater sense of purpose.

Not long after Nava Jeeva Nilayam opened, Ruth Thomas, a Welsh physical therapist, arrived at Vellore and asked to see Paul. She explained that she had been a missionary in China, but the Communist take-over of that country had forced her to flee. While in Hong Kong awaiting a ship to return home to Wales, Ruth heard that a Dr. Brand at Vellore, India, needed help. She immediately changed her plans and sailed to Colombo, Ceylon, and then on to Madras, where she caught the train to Vellore. Ruth was ready and willing to do whatever Paul needed her to do.

Paul was delighted. He put Ruth straight to work. She spent hours at the New Life Center showing the men how to look after themselves. In fact, by the time she was through with them, they knew more about hands and how to care for them than did many surgeons. Although Ruth was shy and modest about her abilities, she was able to draw out the most despondent patients.

One particularly difficult patient Ruth worked hard with was Namo. Namo was studying to become an electrical engineer and had just passed his exams with distinction in 1946, when he was diagnosed with leprosy. Suddenly all his dreams had come crashing down. Namo arrived at the New Life Center in early 1951, despondent and bitter at life and the way people treated him. Ruth worked with Namo, talking with him as she massaged his hands and fingers. Slowly she began to draw him out of his despondency. So impressed was Namo by the love and patience of Ruth and Paul and the other workers at the New Life Center that he decided he wanted to become a Christian. Following his baptism in the Church of South India, Namo decided he'd had enough of his bitterness toward the way society treated him because of his leprosy. Like Ruth, he wanted to have an impact on the lives of other leprosy sufferers.

Ruth began to teach Namo how to care for the hands and feet of leprosy patients. She showed him how to massage patients' hands and fingers to keep them subtle and soft to avoid the hardening and lack of joint movement that came with the onset of the disease. Soon Namo was playing an invaluable role in helping leprosy patients in Vellore.

After one long weekend at the Lady Willingdon Leprosy Sanatorium in Chingleput, Paul returned home feeling sick and tired. It was dark when he entered the house. Margaret asked him to come upstairs so that they could talk away from the children.

"There is a man staying on the veranda," Margaret said. "He has a letter from Dr. Jagadisan, and he came to see you."

Paul felt his heart beat faster. "You mean he has leprosy?" he asked.

"Yes," Margaret replied resolutely.

"But darling," Paul said, "you know children are more susceptible than adults to the bacterium. It's a risk we don't want to take. Why did you invite him here to the house?"

"Well," Margaret began as she turned to face Paul. "My Bible reading on Saturday morning said, 'I was a stranger and you took me in.' He was a stranger. It seemed very clear to me that I should take him in."

Paul could not argue with Margaret's logic. He put his arms around his wife and hugged her. Even though he would have liked nothing better than to crawl into bed, he went downstairs to meet the stranger, whose name was Sadagopan. As Paul examined Sadagopan's leprous hands and feet, he had no way of knowing the stranger that Margaret had welcomed into their lives would one day be an immense help in his research.

For now, however, other matters pressed on Paul, who was due—overdue—for a furlough. Paul found it difficult to imagine leaving his work at the hospital. How could he be idle in England for a whole year when so much had to be done at Vellore? The perfect answer to Paul's dilemma came in the most unexpected way. Early in 1952 Paul learned that the Rockefeller Foundation, based in New York in the United States, had granted him a scholarship. He hadn't even applied for a scholarship with the foundation, but they had heard about his groundbreaking work in leprosy research and had sent a representative to talk to Paul. The rep told Paul, "See anybody you want, anywhere in the world: surgeons, pathologists, leprologists, anyone you think can help you, and take as long as you need. Send us the bills."

This was perhaps the most astonishing news Paul had ever received, and he was overjoyed about the possibilities. Now he could justify being away from Vellore and Nava Jeeva Nilayam for a year. He immediately set about booking tickets for his family of six and making a list of all the specialists he wanted to question. The first leg of Paul's dream come true would be England.

Chapter 13

Hands and Feet

When Paul overheard eight-year-old Christopher talking to his six-year-old sister Jean, he had a sinking feeling that things were not going to be easy for Margaret and the children in England.

"Will there be trees to climb in London?" Jean asked.

"I'm not sure," Christopher replied, "but at least there'll be walls."

Paul thought back to his own transition from India to England, how he and Connie had been let loose upon his two aunts in London. Now Aunt Hope and Aunt Eunice were thirty years older, and four young children were about to descend on them.

Descend they did! Paul was amazed when he found Jean hanging upside down ten feet from the ground on exactly the same lamppost he and Connie had swung from. The aunts had put away their fine china, yet the children managed to demolish several pieces of furniture.

Meanwhile, Paul was scouring England for people who could help him learn better hand surgery techniques. He had brought thousands of postmortem research slides with him and was eager to discuss the surgeries he had performed and learn whether any advances could be made. To that end, he met with Sir Archibald McIndoe, a famous plastic surgeon who had performed complicated surgeries on burned airmen during the war. Paul took hundreds of slides to the meeting, and as he showed them to the surgeon, he explained what he had been doing.

"There's not much I could add," Sir Archibald concluded. "You appear to be up with things, or even more advanced in some cases. I say, every English surgeon should hear what you are pioneering in India. Would you mind frightfully if I put your name in the hat to be a Hunterian lecturer?"

Paul was flabbergasted. He had come to learn from this great surgeon, and instead he was being asked to consider the highest honor any English surgeon could attain. The Hunterian lectureship had been awarded each year by the Royal College of Surgeons since 1805 to encourage the best surgeons in England to discuss their latest research and techniques with their peers.

Since the deadline for choosing the lecturer was looming, Paul rushed back to his aunts' house to write a paper on his leprosy hand surgeries. He was soon informed that he had won the lectureship. He was thrilled to think that he would have the opportunity in late October to illuminate the work done at Vellore to a large group of surgeons from all over the English-speaking world.

October 24, 1952, arrived, and thirty-eight-year-old Paul Brand did his best to conform to the solemnity of the event. The first Hunterian lecturer had stood in the same room at the Royal College and donned the same style of robe since the inauguration of the lectureship. Paul was escorted into the lecture hall by a beadle (official) carrying a gold mace (staff) on a cushion. Not a word was spoken as Paul made a ceremonial bow to his audience and began his lecture. He had been told in advance that there would be no introductions of any kind; his credentials were listed in the program. His sole task was to read his lecture exactly as it appeared on paper. When it was over, he was escorted out in total silence.

Paul had time for conversation once he had taken off his ceremonial robe. He listened eagerly for information that could help him learn more, but everyone agreed that his lecture material was innovative, and they wanted to hear more from him. This both flattered and disappointed Paul. He hoped that he would learn more in America, where his Rockefeller scholarship was soon taking him.

Meanwhile, Margaret, who was still working in the Schell Eye Hospital in Vellore, took some polytechnic college courses in optics and optometry in London to help fill in some of the gaps in her medical knowledge. Given her reluctance to start work at the eye hospital, Margaret was surprised that she now loved working with eye patients. She knew that what she learned on furlough would make her a more competent eye doctor.

In early December 1952, Paul boarded the *Queen Elizabeth II* bound for the United States. He knew that he would not be seeing his family for four months. They would be taking a ship heading to South Africa to spend time with Margaret's parents, who had retired there from England.

The voyage across the Atlantic Ocean was swift. As he sailed westward toward the United States, Paul looked forward to meeting with world-renowned hand surgeons and neurologists in Boston, Chicago, San Francisco, Los Angeles, and New Orleans.

The time sped by as Paul visited these places and shared his knowledge with others. In Boston he met with Dr. Derek Denny-Brown, Harvard professor of neurology. Derek was a New Zealander and a brilliant neurologist and had probably the untidiest office Paul had ever been in. File boxes, papers, X-rays, and books were stacked everywhere. Derek gave Paul his full attention as Paul pulled out slides of damaged nerves of the leprosy patients he had autopsied and asked the neurologist to explain to him what was happening with the nerves. Why had the nerves swelled the way they had? Dr. Denny-Brown pored over the slides under the microscope, carefully examining each slide. "These slides look just like my cats!" the neurologist exclaimed.

Paul looked quizzically at Derek, who went on to explain about some work he had done with cats ten years before. Derek told Paul that he surmised that it wasn't nerve swelling alone that caused damage and paralysis. That occurred only when the swelling was constricted, as it might be by the sheath around the nerve. Such pressure on the nerve would greatly diminish the blood supply and eventually kill the nerve.

Dr. Denny-Brown got out some of his own slides to illustrate what he was talking about. As he and Paul studied the slides under the microscope, the nerve swelling visible on them was identical to that on Paul's slides. It was an enlightening moment for Paul as he thought he was beginning to close in on the cause of the nerve damage that led to paralysis in leprosy patients. But Paul still had unanswered questions, such as why the nerve swelling occurred where it did in the bodies of leprosy patients.

Paul learned from other great doctors in the U.S. cities he visited. In San Francisco he spent two weeks with Dr. Sterling Bunnell, one of the world's leading authorities on hands, whose procedure Paul had followed in his early surgeries on leprosy patients. It was not until he arrived in New Orleans, however, that Paul met the only surgeon outside India who had operated on the hands of leprosy patients. Dr. Daniel Riordan spent one day a week at the only leprosarium in the continental United States, in Carville,

Louisiana. He took Paul with him to the leprosarium, which resembled a small rural town set behind a high wire fence on a loop of the Mississippi River.

At Carville, Paul assisted Dr. Riordan with some hand surgeries and was able to demonstrate some of the techniques he had perfected at Vellore. In turn, Paul observed some useful techniques Dr. Riordan employed in his surgeries. At the end of Paul's visit to New Orleans, Paul and Dr. Riordan agreed to stay in touch.

In New York City, Paul was interviewed on a television program on which he was pleased to promote the medical work being done at Vellore. He was also delighted to show the audience some wooden toys the men at the New Life Center had made.

In April 1953 Paul sailed back to England, where he spent a few days with his aunts in London. During that time he completed conversations he had started with Donald Miller, secretary of the British Mission to Lepers. Paul was now in the forefront of leprosy medicine, and the British Mission to Lepers offered to help support the Brand family financially.

With a happy heart Paul said good-bye to his aunts and boarded his first commercial airplane flight. He was bound for Johannesburg, South Africa, where he would be reunited with Margaret and the children. As he sat in the airplane, Paul looked down first at the European continent and later at the African continent as they passed far below. The trip was long, and Paul was grateful when the airplane touched down in South Africa and he was reunited with his family.

Everyone looked sun-tanned and happy. Paul spent four days with Margaret's parents, and then the Brand family took a two-day train trip to Durban on South Africa's east coast, where they boarded the SS *Karanga* for the trip across the ocean back to India.

On the voyage, Paul had time to tell Margaret about all he had learned during his time in the United States. He was frustrated that he did not have more answers about leprosy but pleased to know that in working in a small Christian hospital in South India, he and his colleagues were performing world-class surgeries.

As the *Karanga* sailed eastward, Paul looked forward to five more years in India. He told himself that perhaps that would be enough time to find the answers he was searching for. It would certainly be long enough for his next project: building a prototype operating room at the New Life Center. Paul already had the plans for it in his head. Instead of purchasing an expensive, foreign operating light, he would make one by hammering a sheet of aluminum into the right shape, polishing it, and attaching it to a two-hundred-watt lightbulb. He imagined suspending the light over a simple wooden operating table with a series of ropes and pulleys.

As soon as he arrived in Vellore, Paul set the men at the New Life Center to work on the project. The men made the operating table, scrubbed out a small room and whitewashed it, made the lamp, and suspended it over the table. On January 30, 1954, Paul performed the first surgery in the small operating theater. It should have been a day of celebration, but the day turned to tragedy. Twelve members of the Vellore facility were on their way to a picnic when their station wagon crashed and flipped over. Paul raced to the hospital, where he helped to evaluate and operate on the accident victims.

Thankfully, no one was killed in the accident, but one of Paul's favorite former students, Dr. Mary Verghese, was paralyzed from the waist down, and her face was horribly disfigured. Paul was distraught when he saw her, but he vowed to do everything he could to help Mary find a new path.

Mary spent many months in a rotating bed in the hospital. Sometimes she was right side up, and sometimes she was tilted to one side or the other, or even upside down. Whatever position she was in, Paul spent hours squatting beside her, talking to her about her faith in Christ, and encouraging her in her recovery.

Eventually Paul was able to fuse some of the bones in Mary's back so that she could sit in a wheelchair. Now Paul's real challenge began. He encouraged Mary to help him evaluate leprosy patients, and one day he suggested that she learn how to do hand surgery.

"Surgery!" she protested. "Have you forgotten, Dr. Brand? I am a paraplegic!"

Paul laughed. "But Mary, this is one of the few operations you *have* to perform sitting down," he countered.

Over the next months, Paul and Mary spent many hours operating together in the tiny theater at the

New Life Center. Every time Paul watched the ador-
ing way the leprosy patients listened to this Indian
woman doctor in a wheelchair, he thanked God that
he had been allowed to play a part in Mary's remarkable recovery and transformation into a gifted hand
surgeon.

While Paul was set to prove with his prototype
operating theater that sophisticated surgery could
be done under simple, rural conditions, his influence
was spreading around the world. In October 1954 he
was invited to visit a hospital in North India where
several of his former students were working. After
that he was invited to Calcutta to deliver a series of
lectures at the Calcutta School of Tropical Medicine.
The net was cast wider when the government of
Nigeria asked him to visit and demonstrate his surgery techniques on leprosy patients.

Paul set off on this adventure, glad that he would
get to see his sister Connie and brother-in-law David
Wilmshurst, who were serving as missionaries in
Gindiri, Nigeria. He also relished spending time with
his African counterpart, John Dreisbach, an American doctor based in Kano who was ahead of Vellore
in the care of leprosy patients' feet.

When Paul returned home, he was determined to
take what Dr. Dreisbach had shown him and improve
on it. From the time he had started making regular
visits to the leprosarium in Chingleput, he had been
aware that shoes were a problem for leprosy patients.
One day Paul had found a pair of sandals outside the
hut where patients were having the ulcers on their
feet dressed. As he examined the sandals he was

horrified to see nails sticking up through the soles. Paul took the sandals inside and found their owner. Sure enough, the ulcers on the man's foot matched perfectly with the nails sticking up through the sandals. The patient had not even realized the nails were there! Paul now knew that he would have to focus more on feet and on helping leprosy patients take better care of them.

In Kano, Nigeria, John Dreisbach had shown Paul how they were making shoes fitted to the patients' feet. The shoes offered good support and protection as well as a level of comfort that reduced the pressure spots. Paul began experimenting with shoes fitted to leprosy patients' feet. His helper, or test patient, in this was Sadagopan, whom Margaret had invited to their home on College Hill and whom Paul had first met on the veranda. Sadagopan began wearing the various styles Paul made, from wooden clogs to molded rubber shoes. He would happily wear the shoes for days, weeks, sometimes months, without getting any ulcers. But when Sadagopan eventually did get ulcers, Paul would modify the shoes, which Sadagopan would then begin wearing.

Paul worked at the process methodically, just as he had when studying the hands of leprosy patients. He came to realize that the perfect shoe for his patients needed both a soft, pliable innersole that could adapt to the contour of the foot and a well-constructed outer shoe that gave good protection and support. He imported several pairs of a new microcellular rubber sandal called a thong that was popular in Hawaii. He used the base of the thongs to craft innersoles, and when he was convinced he was on the right track, he traveled to Calcutta to meet with representatives from Bata, a large shoe manufacturer. The company agreed to work with Paul, mixing various batches of microcellular rubber in differing degrees of softness until they settled on the right rubber mix for the job.

At the same time, "Uncle Robbie" Robertson showed up in Vellore. Dr. Robertson was a recently retired orthopedic surgeon in charge of prosthetic workshops in New Zealand. He had arrived to live out the rest of his days at Vellore helping people. Paul put him to work on shoes for leprosy patients. A patient and gifted man, Uncle Robbie was soon fashioning leather shoes shaped to the contour of a patient's foot. Paul marveled at the workmanship of each pair of shoes the orthopedic surgeon made.

Not long after Uncle Robbie arrived, John Girling showed up at Paul's door. He was a young Englishman disillusioned with British society and was traveling the world to find something meaningful in his life. He offered to do anything Paul wanted him to do to help leprosy patients. All Paul could offer him in return was the paltry sum of one hundred rupees a month for his labor. John jumped at the opportunity. Soon he was hard at work making shoes. In fact, in no time at all he was a recognized expert in making custom shoes for leprosy patients.

Eventually it was determined that the best kind of sole for these shoes was one that was slightly curved long ways, causing the patient's foot to roll forward as the person walked. This seemed to produce the least amount of rubbing on the foot and so lessened the chance of ulcers forming. The design had just one drawback: it was easy for the wearer to twist over sideways onto his ankles, causing torn ligaments and sometimes fractures. Careful instruction in how to walk in the shoes had to be given to those who wore them. All the while Sadagopan continued to work with Paul, trying out all sorts of new shoe designs and styles.

While new people were showing up to work with Paul and his team at Vellore, the Brand family was changing and expanding. Christopher was enrolled in boarding school in the Nilgiri Hills in Ootaca-mund, a town not far from Kotagiri, where he was used to spending the hot season. Margaret gave birth to another baby, a fourth daughter, whom they named Patricia.

The slow, methodical work of improving the lives of leprosy patients and many others continued. Paul often thought back to what he had learned on his trip to Africa. He wished he had a better way to share his team's latest findings with isolated doctors work-ing with leprosy patients. When Paul met Carlo and Paxey Marconi, a motion picture producer and his wife from Bombay, he asked them to extend their filmmaking expertise to make a movie about the work with leprosy patients at Vellore and the New Life Center. The Marconis agreed. Paul and Paxey wrote the script, and Carlo directed and filmed the movie, *Lifted Hands*. Paul was very satisfied with the end result. He then suggested that Carlo film one of Paul's hand surgeries. Later, while Paul performed a tendon-free graft on a patient, Carlo filmed every facet of the surgery.

By the time the Brand family was ready for another furlough at the end of 1957, Paul had two movies to take along—and a fifth baby daughter, his namesake, Pauline, who was born at Vellore on December 2, 1957. Paul's mother arrived to see the family off on furlough. She was now a wrinkled, bent-over old woman of seventy-eight, a self-supporting missionary living her dream of reaching the hill tribes people of southern India. Sometimes she would bring a leprosy patient down to Vellore for Paul to treat, but she never stayed long, telling him that she had to get back because she had too much work to do.

As his family climbed aboard the ship for the trip home, Paul wondered whether England was ready for six Brand children.

Honors and Awards

Three weeks after setting out from India, the Brand family arrived back in England in early 1958. On a freezing cold evening in London, Paul stood at the door of Pilgrim Lodge, the home recently bought and redecorated by the Mission to Lepers for use as a home for furloughing missionaries. Paul groaned inwardly as he surveyed the newly wallpapered rooms and noted the pride in the live-in caretaker's voice. He had a sinking feeling that staying at Pilgrim Lodge would not be an easy transition for the children. After all, they were used to climbing in and out of windows and dangling from parapets at home in Vellore. Thankfully, none of the children did any serious damage to the place. Three-year-old Patricia did manage to draw a "mural" with black crayon on the wallpaper in the living room, and the older children played pranks involving the telephone.

Once back in England, Margaret was left to deal with finding boarding schools for Christopher and Jean and the daily care of the children, while Paul embarked on a rigorous speaking tour. He was determined to help English doctors and Christian groups understand the progress being made in leprosy care and to explain how much more still needed to be done.

One of the things that helped Paul spread the message was the film of him performing the tendon-free graft surgery on a patient's hand. Paul showed the footage at a meeting of the British Orthopedic Association. The film was a big hit; everyone seemed to want a copy. Soon copies of the film were made and translated into four languages. Medical libraries around the world began requesting copies.

As a result of the film, Paul's message was being carried farther than he could have dreamed. The film was entered in various contests and festivals. It placed second in the British Medical Association contest, placed first in the German equivalent, and took first place at the Milan Film Festival in the technical films category. Paul—or his hands at least—was a movie star!

As the time back in England on furlough sped by, the Brand family, minus fourteen-year-old Christopher and twelve-year-old Jean, were ready to return to Vellore. Paul was conflicted about leaving two of his children behind in England at boarding school.

Although it was accepted that British children whose parents lived overseas would return to England for their education, Paul recalled how hard it had been for him to be separated from his parents. He also remembered that he had never seen his father again. Nevertheless, he and Margaret had agreed that it was the best choice for their two oldest children. With heavy hearts Paul and Margaret said their good-byes to Christopher and Jean and returned to India with the rest of the family.

Paul knew that with his return to the Christian Medical College and Hospital, his role would be changing. During his time at the hospital, he had performed about five thousand reconstructive surgeries on the hands and feet of leprosy patients. Paul had directly performed half the surgeries and had supervised his students as they did the other half. In his absence on furlough, some of the students he had trained proved capable of taking on a full surgery load. It was time for Paul to accept his role on the world stage with regard to the treatment of leprosy. A week after the family arrived back in Vellore, Paul set out for Japan to attend the Seventh International Congress on Leprology.

At the congress Paul challenged leprosy experts to include surgery and rehabilitation in all their treatment programs. "To be cured of active leprosy but left with crippled hands and feet may be a victory over the bacillus, but it is a defeat for the man," he declared.

On his way back to Vellore, Paul stopped off in Hong Kong, where he met with Dr. Howard Rusk, who was also visiting the city. Dr. Rusk was an American doctor from New York City who was a passionate pioneer for the disabled. As the two doctors discussed disabilities and rehabilitation, Paul wished that Mary Verghese could meet Dr. Rusk. He felt sure that the two of them would get along well and inspire each other to new ventures.

At the hospital in Vellore, the leprosy work attracted a steady stream of visitors wanting to learn from Paul and his team. People came from as far as Switzerland and the Canary Islands. A succession of American surgeons also came to work with Paul, who was constantly teaching and learning from other surgeons, exchanging knowledge that helped to solve the problems they all encountered.

One of Paul's dreams came true when Mary Verghese sought his advice. Mary told Paul that she longed to study rehabilitation techniques under Dr. Howard Rusk in New York. However, she was nervous about traveling overseas in her wheelchair and fitting into the program with her disability. She told Paul that she would love to come back to Vellore and become the director of a rehabilitation department— something that did not yet exist there.

Paul encouraged her. "I think if you believe that this is something God wants you to do, nothing on earth is going to stop you," he told Mary.

Mary beamed. She applied to the postgraduate program studying under Dr. Rusk and was accepted. Paul was delighted to see someone he had encouraged, a woman in a wheelchair no less, taking such a big step. He encouraged Mary at her farewell in December 1959 before her departure for New York City by saying, "Because Mary has lost the ability to walk, but not her courage and devotion, who knows how many hundreds of others will be able to stand and walk and run on good, strong limbs."

Five months after Mary's farewell, on the afternoon of May 24, 1960, Paul was working at the hospital and received a telegraph consisting of four simple words. Those words had a profound effect on everyone at Vellore: "Aunt Ida has gone."

When he heard the news, tears began to stream down Paul's face. Dr. Ida Scudder, founder of the Christian Medical College and Hospital, was dead at the age of ninety. Paul bowed his head and thought about his dear friend who had been so encouraging of his work over the years. He thought of the many times she had sat through his hand surgeries, holding the patient's other hand and reassuring the patient while Paul operated. He would miss her, and he knew that everyone else at Vellore would also miss her.

Ida's funeral service was held in front of the main administration block at the hospital, as there was no building big enough to contain the huge crowd that gathered. It seemed as though the whole town of Vellore had come to pay their last respects to a woman who had greatly affected their town and their lives. Paul was asked to give a eulogy at the funeral service. He chose as the text for his remarks Joshua 1:2: "Moses My servant is dead. Now therefore, arise, go over this Jordan."

As Ida's body was buried beside that of her mother, Paul reflected on the woman's amazing achievements. In sixty years, Ida's work at Vellore had grown from a small dispensary to a huge, modern hospital that treated tens of thousands of patients each year. The hospital employed 735 doctors, nurses, and technicians, most of whom were Indian and worked side by side with fifty overseas staff from more than six countries. The medical college had 795 students in training who were studying medicine, nursing, pharmacy, pathology, radiology, laboratory services, and public health.

Two months after Ida's funeral, Paul was on the road again. This time he had been invited to Geneva, Switzerland, for three weeks to write informational pamphlets on leprosy treatment for use in World Health Organization programs around the world.

From Geneva, Paul traveled to New York City to receive the prestigious Albert Lasker Award for outstanding leadership and service in the world of rehabilitation. Paul was embarrassed by such personal accolades, but he realized that accepting the award would raise the awareness of leprosy rehabilitation around the world, and he was grateful for that.

While in New York, Paul visited Mary Verghese and was glad to see that she was thriving in the big city and eager to bring the new things she was learning home to Vellore.

From New York, it was on to Sweden to meet with the Swedish Red Cross. After Paul spoke with the organization, the Red Cross made a large donation to help bring rehabilitation to patients in their own homes. This was another of Paul's dreams come true.

From Europe, Paul hurried home to host the ten-day Scientific Meeting on Rehabilitation in Leprosy, held in Vellore in November 1960. The conference was organized in conjunction with the World Health Organization, the Leonard Wood Memorial Foundation, the International Society for Rehabilitation of the Disabled, and the Vellore Christian Medical College. For Paul this was yet another dream come true. Gathered in one place were some of the world's leading experts on leprosy and surgery. Many helpful discussions along with surgical and rehabilitative demonstrations took place throughout the conference. Paul and his team of researchers were able to present many of their findings regarding leprosy and its treatment. The detailed research records from the Vellore team stunned the conference attendees. The team presented copious notes and records of every single surgery they had performed, accompanied by a series of photographs before and after the procedure and during the rehabilitation process.

Paul was particularly pleased with two outcomes of the conference. First, the conference unanimously agreed that the lack of nerve sensation in leprosy sufferers should be classified as a major disability. The conference also strongly recommended that from that time on, leprosy should be treated like other diseases and studied in institutions where the medical field could bring expertise to bear. Leprosy had moved beyond the prejudice that had existed toward the disease for centuries. Now it was to be treated like any other debilitating disease, with ongoing research into more effective treatments and rehabilitation practices. Paul could not have asked for a better outcome as he thought back to thirteen years before when Robert Cochrane had told him of the total lack of research on the disease.

That Christmas Paul and Margaret decided to take their children to visit Granny Brand, who was living in the Kalrayan Hills, about one hundred miles southwest of Vellore. Getting to her place was quite an adventure. First they drove to the end of the road. Then they transferred to a Jeep that took them over rough tracks to the foothills of the mountains. From there it was another eighteen miles up into the mountains to Granny Brand's house. Granny had sent down her pony and some men from the village with a *dholi*—a sheet of canvas slung between two bamboo poles—to meet the family at the end of the Jeep track. The two youngest children, Patricia and Pauline, rode in the *dholi* carried on the shoulders of four men. Margaret, Mary, and Estelle took turns riding Granny's pony, while Paul walked all the way. It was a steep climb up into the hills, and the higher they climbed, the cooler the temperature got. The family finally rounded a bend in the path, where a group of villagers were waiting to welcome them and escort them to Granny Brand's small house.

Christmas dinner with Granny was very different. Even though Paul and Margaret had brought a fully cooked turkey and all the trimmings from Madras, the family did not get to gather around the table and eat it together. Just before they were due to serve the meal, a woman critically ill with typhoid was carried to Granny's house. Granny took one look at the woman and dropped everything, spending the rest of the evening and late into the night tending to her.

Meanwhile, the rest of the Brand family ate Christmas dinner without Paul's mother. Paul realized that his mother was just as feisty as she had ever been. He knew she would never come down from the mountains to live, and that one day he would receive word that she had died there.

The trip to the Kalrayan Hills to visit Granny Brand was a refreshing break, but straight after Christmas, Paul plunged back into a heavy work and travel schedule. In January 1961 the American Society for Surgery of the Hand flew him all the way from Vellore to Miami, Florida, to be the keynote speaker at their conference.

No sooner had Paul arrived back in Vellore from his trip to the United States than he and Margaret were invited to be one of three couples to be introduced to Queen Elizabeth II on her visit to Madras. Again, Paul was grateful for the opportunity to speak a little about his work. What he spoke about must have impressed the queen, because not long afterward Paul received an official letter informing him that she had granted him a CBE (Commander of the British Empire), an honor one step below knighthood.

For the honor granted to be valid, it had to be accepted within a year at an investiture ceremony.

These ceremonies were held four times a year in England, but none of the dates coincided with Paul's travels. The honor would have to be conferred by the British high commissioner to India, who rarely came to Madras. Paul wrote to the deputy commissioner in Madras to see whether he could do the investiture and bestow the honor on him. The deputy commissioner wrote to say that he could and that Paul should plan on staying for lunch when he came.

On the investiture day, Paul was flying back to Madras from northern India. When he arrived at the airport, his suit was creased and wrinkled from sleeping on the airplane. He did his best to pat it down as he headed to the government house. Paul was expecting a small, quick ceremony with the deputy commissioner and then a cup of tea and sandwiches for lunch. Much to his surprise, when he arrived at the government house, he found the place draped in flags, with limousines parked outside. Paul was bewildered and wondered whether he had mixed up the time or the date for his investiture. Inside he found the political and social elites of Madras as well as many of his colleagues from the hospital in Vellore waiting for him. The men were dressed in morning suits and the women in fine dresses, their necks draped with jewelry. Paul suddenly realized everyone was there for *him*. He felt self-conscious in his wrinkled suit, and more so when one of his Indian colleagues stepped forward to remove a bedbug from his suit coat.

Following the investiture ceremony, a formal banquet was held, with Paul seated between the deputy commissioner and the mayor of Madras. It was hard for Paul to grasp that it was all being done in honor of him.

Paul now anticipated the joy of dedicating the new medicine and rehabilitation building in Vellore in January 1963. The building was one of the first such facilities in India. Dr. Sarvapalli Radhakrishnan, president of India, was present for the dedication. Dr. Mary Verghese, whose dream of such a facility in Vellore had come true, sat beaming beside Paul throughout the ceremony. One of the most wonderful things about the new building was that it was not just for leprosy patients. The walls of fear and ignorance toward the disease were crumbling, and leprosy patients would be treated in the facility along with other patients.

Although Paul enthusiastically endorsed rehabilitation—and many men and women had been rehabilitated at Vellore over the years—he was concerned for the plight of the deformed and crippled in India, who most often ended up as beggars or being taken care of by their families. What these people needed was meaningful work that could bring purpose to their daily existence. Paul talked to several businessmen about the situation, and together they formed the Abilities Trust. The aim of the trust was to oversee the development of factories that employed only disabled people. Before long the first factory was up and running. It employed fifty disabled people who worked at manufacturing typewriter parts. The new venture was so successful that other factories soon followed.

With the end of their third term as missionaries at Vellore in sight, Paul and Margaret began to discuss what they should do next. Sixteen years earlier Paul had left England to come to Vellore and help the medical college gain accreditation from the Indian government. The Christian Medical College and Hospital at Vellore was now considered one of the best institutions in Asia, with the most up-to-date leprosy treatments available anywhere in the world. Paul began to feel that God wanted him to move on. He knew that he would always be a part of the community of those who worked to improve the lives of leprosy patients around the world. He just did not know exactly how his and Margaret's future would unfold.

Change

In April 1963, the Brands once again boarded a ship, this time the *Cilicia*, for the trip back to London, England. Once they had settled in, the children were enrolled in school. Patricia and Pauline went to a local school; Estelle, to a school across the city, which required a daily train commute; and Mary, to the same boarding school that Jean attended.

Paul and Margaret now met with leaders of the Mission to Lepers. They agreed to continue serving with the mission, with Paul as their spokesperson and liaison with other organizations, such as the World Health Organization. As spokesperson for the mission, Paul agreed to spend a year traveling the world, speaking and teaching.

Before he set out on his new task, Paul spent the summer with the children. The entire family toured France and Switzerland by car, camping along the way and enjoying each other's company.

In September, Paul was off on his world tour. Jean, who had just finished boarding school, offered to look after the two youngest children so that Margaret could join Paul for the first part of the tour. Their first stop was Rio de Janeiro, Brazil, for the International Congress on Leprosy. At the congress, Paul sat proudly and listened as Margaret presented a paper on her work with eye patients, with special emphasis on treating those whose eyesight had been damaged by leprosy. Margaret's years of methodical research at the Schell Eye Hospital in Vellore had made her a world authority on the subject.

Following the conference, Paul and Margaret traveled to leprosy hospitals and clinics throughout South America and then up the East Coast of the United States. In Montreal, Canada, they enjoyed a few days together relaxing before Margaret headed back to England to take care of the children.

Paul continued visiting clinics and hospitals and talking on radio shows, at Rotary Groups, and at church gatherings across the United States and Canada. Everywhere he went he found people whom he had trained or worked with at Vellore. Then it was on to Africa, Australia, New Guinea, Borneo, and Thailand. Lastly, he returned to Vellore to check on the work there and to visit his mother, who was still going strong and living by herself in the Kalrayan Hills.

Paul arrived back in England exhausted but exhilarated. He loved being a point person for leprosy—observing techniques on one continent and demonstrating them on the next. The lack of understanding about leprosy was shrinking as more experts gave the disease the attention it deserved.

The next year Paul followed a similar path, spending time in Caracas, Venezuela; Addis Ababa, Ethiopia; and Vellore. He enjoyed the challenge of it all, but he wondered how many more years he could keep up such a hectic pace. Paul thought about getting a permanent job as a surgeon in England. In fact, he had been offered several positions, but he couldn't imagine restricting his leprosy work around the world.

In 1965, just as he and Margaret were praying about what they should do next, Paul happened to visit the leprosarium in Carville, Louisiana. He gave a series of lectures on what he had learned about rehabilitation through working at Vellore. Afterward, the director of the facility, Dr. Edgar Johnwick, approached Paul. "Here at Carville we've never had a pattern of rehabilitation like that!" he exclaimed. "It astonishes me that your patients in India have a better level of care than ours do here in the United States. You must move here and become head of surgery and rehabilitation and show us how you do it!"

Paul wondered whether Dr. Johnwick was joking, but the doctor looked very serious, and very excited. "Would my English qualifications be accepted here?" he asked.

"I'm sure we could arrange that," Dr. Johnwick said.

Paul was taken aback, but he felt like he should continue the conversation. "And how about my wife, Margaret. As you know, she is an eye specialist. Could she work at Carville?"

"I don't see why not," Dr. Johnwick answered.

Paul had one last question. "Could I have as much time off as I needed to continue my leprosy work around the world?"

"Absolutely," the director stated.

That night as Paul lay in bed at the guesthouse just a stone's throw from the Mississippi River, he tried to imagine his family living in Carville. There were wide-open spaces, and Dr. Johnwick had said that the girls could fix up the dilapidated stables if they wanted to keep horses. Louisiana State University was located just forty-five minutes away in Baton Rouge. Christopher might like to attend there.

The next morning Paul asked a staff member if he could borrow a reel-to-reel tape recorder. He sat in his room, turned the record knob, and spoke into the microphone. "Hello, everyone," he began. "I'm here in Carville, and a very interesting opportunity has come up. I can't possibly take a serious look at it until I have heard from all of you." Only two years after returning to England "for good," Paul was outlining the pros and cons of moving to Carville.

Paul mailed off the tape to England and continued his travels. It was two months before he returned to England, and upon his arrival, his family informed him that they had made a decision: if Paul wanted to go to Carville, then they were up for the challenge. It would mean separating again, but hopefully within a year or two they could all be together again in the United States.

Paul's cousin, John Harris, and his family were home in England on furlough, and they agreed to take in several members of the Brand family. Jean, who was now training to be a nurse, could stay with them on her weekends off. Estelle had one more year of high school, which she wanted to complete in England before moving to the United States. Mary was still at boarding school and would come back to the Harrises for holidays. Christopher would go on ahead, tour the United States by bus, and enroll at Louisiana State University in the fall.

Paul felt strongly that God had arranged the circumstances for him to go to Carville, so with peace in his heart, he called Dr. Johnwick and agreed to begin work at the leprosarium in December 1965. Not long afterward Paul received word that Dr. Johnwick had died suddenly. He was sorry that he would not have the opportunity to work with such a gifted man as Edgar Johnwick, but Paul felt sure that his replacement would be just as forward thinking with regard to the treatment of leprosy.

Paul left England ahead of the rest of his family and arrived in Carville in late December. It was wintertime in Louisiana, but compared to winter in England, it felt positively balmy.

The leprosarium at Carville was administered and run by the U.S. Public Health Service. It was situated on 330 acres of land beside the Mississippi

River, ninety miles west of New Orleans and thirty miles south of Baton Rouge. From his previous visits Paul was already familiar with the lay of the land. The property was completely enclosed with a high wire mesh fence and a guardhouse, and guards controlled all entry to and exit from the facility. The site had once been a plantation. Immediately inside the gate to the right was the old plantation house that had been converted to administrative offices. Beyond the old plantation house sat the two-story hospital building with various wings branching off from it. Beyond the hospital building was a large expanse of open grass fields crisscrossed by concrete paths. There was even a small lake on the property for fishing. Nestled between the hospital building and the field were small bungalows that were home to many of the lifelong patients. And live oak trees grew everywhere, spreading their branches wide and offering shade from the fierce bayou summer heat.

On the left side of the entrance gate were two streets about a block long and running parallel to each other. Along these two streets sat neat, clapboard staff houses, shaded by more towering live oak trees. Upon his arrival in Carville, Paul was shown to a large four-bedroom house on the first street. The rambling house had been built in the 1920s and had large windows that could open wide, high ceilings, and a veranda on either side. Paul decided it would be the perfect place for his family.

After he had moved in, Paul acquainted himself with more of the history of his new home. In the early

1890s the Louisiana legislature had decreed that the old, rundown plantation in Carville would be the new home for citizens with leprosy. The first seven patients were brought to the site hidden on a coal barge from New Orleans, as it was illegal for anyone with leprosy to ride on public transportation. Those patients moved into the old, crumbling slave quarters that were infested with bats, malarial mosquitoes, and snakes.

No one was willing to move to Carville and care for the leprosy patients there, until four nuns from the Daughters of Charity took up the challenge. They cared for the patients, whose number continued to grow steadily, and worked hard to clear land and repair the dilapidated buildings. Eventually the U.S. Public Health Service took over the facility, but the nuns remained and continued to work tirelessly.

Over the years, great strides had been taken in the care of leprosy patients at Carville. Paul noted that it had been the first institution in the world to begin using the relatively new sulfone drugs to treat leprosy. Even in the progressive United States, however, leprosy patients faced many of the same prejudices as those with the disease in India and other parts of the world. Once a patient arrived at the facility, he or she was not allowed to leave. Barbed wire was strung along the top of the fence, and guard towers were installed to stop patients from trying to escape. Newly arrived patients were told to sever ties to their families, and those who were married were encouraged to divorce and let their spouse go on with his or her life. All those who arrived at Carville as patients had their civil rights revoked and were not allowed to vote.

Paul was glad to learn that things had begun to change during the 1950s. The barbed wire was removed, the guard towers were torn down, and patients were given back their civil rights. With the use of new drugs to kill the leprosy bacilli and arrest the spread of the disease, patients were no longer required to live at the institution, though many still chose to do so. After all, some of the patients had spent thirty or more years living at Carville. The institution was home to them, and they had nowhere else to go.

Paul was settled into the house by the time Margaret and the youngest two girls, eleven-year-old Patricia and eight-year-old Pauline, arrived at Carville in January 1966. Patricia and Pauline immediately began collecting pets. Before Paul knew it, he was sharing his house with a cat and kittens, a collie dog and her puppies, and Simon, an inquisitive baby skunk! Meanwhile, Peanut—the pony—lived in the stable out back.

Paul soon learned of an unfortunate consequence to Dr. Johnwick's sudden death. The staff surgeon at the facility apparently did not want to lose his position in the department and had persuaded Johnwick's replacement to withdraw the offer for Paul to be head of surgery. Instead, Paul was instructed that he could work only as the head of rehabilitation.

At first this devastated Paul, who had been a surgeon for twenty years, was world-renowned in the field, and had lectured all over the globe on surgical practices. Paul had even turned down an offer to be groomed for the position as head of surgery at the Royal National Orthopedic Hospital in London because it would not allow him to continue his leprosy work. For similar reasons he had also turned down an offer to become chairman of Orthopedics at Stanford University medical school in California. Paul took a deep breath and decided to trust God to work out the situation.

Chapter 16

Carville

"You have to visit Stanley Stein," Paul's assistant told him soon after his arrival at Carville. "He's a legend here."

Paul smiled. "And at Vellore too!" he replied. "We always looked forward to getting *The Star* newspaper. What an honor it will be to meet the man who started it."

The assistant grimaced. "Unfortunately, he can't write anymore. In fact, there's not much he can do for himself. He kept the newspaper up after he went blind, but now he's pretty deaf as well. Still, he has a wonderful spirit about him."

"How long has he been here?" Paul inquired.

"Since 1930, you know, the bad old days, when people with Hansen's disease (leprosy) came for life. Of course, Stanley isn't his real name, either. He changed that the day he arrived so that he wouldn't cast shame on his family."

Paul sighed. Whether in India, Ethiopia, or the United States, the story of leprosy was always one of shame and isolation.

Later that day, Paul made his way to Stanley's small room. Stanley was sitting in a chair by his bed, and Paul could immediately see the scar tissue on his hands and feet from years of constant injury resulting from his lack of feeling. Although Stanley could not see Paul because of his blindness, the two men were able to communicate if Paul got close to him and talked directly into Stanley's hearing aid. Paul found Stanley to be a warm and generous person with a sharp mind and a great wit. Stanley told Paul all sorts of stories about Carville's past and inquired of Paul about all the latest medical breakthroughs in the treatment of leprosy, which at Carville was called by its new name, Hansen's disease.

Paul was grateful that things were changing fast for leprosy patients. With proper care and regular checkups there was no reason for any leprosy patient to go blind or lose the use of his or her hands and feet. It was the beginning of a new era in the treatment of Hansen's disease, but for Stanley Stein many of these breakthroughs had come too late. Stanley's hearing was failing fast, and he was slowly losing the ability to know whether anyone was even in the room with him. Before long his keen mind would be trapped in a body that offered it no sensorial feedback. Leprosy had robbed Stanley of the ability to feel anything through his skin on over 90 percent of his body. His mind would be alive but totally cut off from the rest of the world. Within a short time of Paul's arrival at Carville, that is indeed what happened. It was heartbreaking for Paul to watch and realize there was nothing more he or anyone else could do for Stanley, who died in 1967, lost inside his own silent world.

Paul found it difficult to accept the level of prejudice that until recently had existed against leprosy patients in such a modern country. Yet after their move to Carville, the Brand family came face-to-face with another kind of prejudice: racism. While living in India, Indians surrounded the Brands; they had filled every function in society. The children had Indian nannies, and the family had an Indian cook and housekeeper. Indians also worked alongside Paul and Margaret at the hospital and medical college as colleagues and often as their supervisors. The whole family, and most of the faculty at Vellore, did not think of the color of a person's skin as a factor in how they related to the person. Not so in the Deep South of the United States in 1966. The Civil Rights Act had been passed by Congress in 1964, which banned discrimination based on race, color, religion, or national origin in employment practices and public accommodations; and the Voting Rights Act had been passed in 1965 to outlaw discriminatory voting practices that disenfranchised African Americans. Martin Luther King Jr. continued to push for complete equality between blacks and whites. Yet racism in the South remained an enormous problem. While Hansen's disease was a great leveler of people, outside the confines of the leprosarium at Carville, things were different. Paul was shocked to learn that when he went out the front gate of the institution, turned left, and walked a few hundred yards, he was in one of the poorest rural black communities in the South. The town of Carville consisted of rundown shacks without electricity or running water. Any poor person in India would have felt right at home in one of them.

The two youngest Brands, Patricia and Pauline, bore the brunt of the social upheaval. They were enrolled in public school. However, in Louisiana, public schools were still segregated. The bus would pick the girls up each morning at the leprosarium gate and take them to the all white school in St. Gabriel, the next town from Carville. Meanwhile, the black children from the town of Carville were taken to Sunshine School in the next town beyond St. Gabriel. After the schools were desegregated, Patricia and Pauline had to endure many uncomfortable situations as black and white students learned to accept each other's presence and get along. Paul was concerned for his daughters at school as they dealt with the upheaval of desegregation, but he had faith that they would work things out for themselves. Meanwhile, much work was to be done at the leprosarium in Carville.

The situation regarding Paul's position at Carville eventually remedied itself. One of the assistant directors at the institution had taken a personal interest in the matter and lobbied the U.S. Public Health Service headquarters in Washington, D.C., to give Carville the benefit of Paul's specialized surgical abilities. In 1968 Paul was made Director of Surgery while retaining his responsibilities as Director of Rehabilitation. Now Paul was enjoying rehabilitation more than anything else. On the surgery side he mostly acted as a consultant to the staff surgeons and performed difficult surgeries when they came along. Having performed surgeries sometimes morning, noon, and night at Vellore, he liked the easier pace at Carville. Besides, his work on the rehabilitation side was about to get a lot busier.

Paul had met Mary Switzer when he received the Lasker Award in New York City eight years before. Mary had also been a recipient of the award at the same ceremony. She was now the Commissioner of the Department of Vocational Rehabilitation for the Department of Health, Education, and Welfare. When she learned that Paul Brand was working for the U.S. Public Health Service at Carville, she visited him. As she and Paul talked, Mary became very excited about what Paul was trying to achieve at Carville. In fact, she became a staunch ally and, because of her position in Washington, D.C., told Paul, "Whatever you need for your research, just ask."

Paul knew she meant it. How he would have loved to have heard those words back in Vellore when money for research was in such short supply. He didn't waste any time in taking Mary up on her offer.

He already had his eye on a new piece of technology that he had a hunch could significantly improve the lives of leprosy patients.

Soon a forty-thousand dollar thermography machine was installed in Paul's clinic at Carville. The machine was able to measure the variance in temperature in a patient's hands and feet. While in India, Paul had taught himself by just using his hand to tell whether a patient had a patch of skin where the temperature was higher than the surrounding tissue. This was important because an increase in temperature showed areas of stress and possible tissue damage long before it broke through the skin and became visible to the naked eye.

The thermography machine was accurate at detecting as little as a quarter of a degree temperature difference. The machine presented a thermograph of the hand or foot on a screen, and a hard copy could be printed that showed pictorial temperature differentials. The cool areas of the skin would show up as green or blue, with warmer areas ascending through violet, orange, red, and yellow, and the hottest areas would show up as white.

When Paul studied a thermograph and noticed hot spots on the readout, he could stop further damage or infected ulcers from rupturing the skin. The thermography machine became an effective tool in early detection and treatment of tissue.

Although thermography was a useful tool, it did not answer Paul's burning question: Why could a normal person walk for an hour or more and suffer no damage to his or her feet, when a leprosy patient, even one who had undergone corrective foot surgery, doing the same would almost always end up with tissue damage and ulcers? That is where Paul came up with the idea of slipper socks to help him unlock the mystery.

Paul approached a chemical company to produce small microcapsules containing dye. The microcapsules had a skin of heavy wax that with constant pressure would ultimately break down and release the dye. These microcapsules were then impregnated into foam socks that a person slipped onto his or her feet, hence slipper socks. Once the chemical company perfected the microcapsules, Paul had a machine built at Carville to produce them, and then the leprosy patients got to work making slipper socks.

As a person walked in the socks, microcapsules would rupture at pressure points on the feet, and the dye would be released into the foam, turning blue as it did so. The more microcapsules that ruptured, the darker the blue dye. After testing the socks with his staff, Paul was satisfied that they worked as they were supposed to, and he went to work on his research. One of the physical therapists at the hospital volunteered to walk eight miles around the concrete-floored corridors of the institution. After every two miles he would change his slipper socks, and Paul would take a thermograph of his feet.

At the end of the experiment, Paul was fascinated by the results. After two miles, it was clear from the thermograph and the dye on the socks that the

pressure points had been on the big toe and the inner
edge of the physical therapist's foot. However, after
the next two miles, the pressure points had shifted
to the outside of the foot. For each of the four thermographs and socks, there was a different pressure
point on the foot. While he did not make any of his
leprosy patients walk the eight miles to repeat the
experiment, Paul had enough of his patients wear
the slipper socks that over time he began to clearly
see what was going on. It was clear from the physical
therapist's results that as he walked, he was changing his gait to relieve pressure points on the feet and
avoid blisters and tissue damage. Paul realized that
he himself did the same thing when he walked, not
consciously but subconsciously. As the nerves sent
pain signals to the brain, the brain would adjust his
gait to alleviate the pain signals and shift the load
to other pressure points. It was a simple and natural
process to avoid injury to the feet.

As Paul examined the slipper socks of leprosy
patients, he saw that the patients never altered their
gait, no matter how far they walked. They walked on
the same pressure points on their feet, and this led to
tissue damage and the formation of ulcers. Because
of nerve damage, no nervous system process allowed
them to respond to pain signals and adjust their gait.
And with no pain signals getting through their nerves
to the brain, the brain was mistakenly led to believe
that their feet were injury free.

This was a moment of clarity and understanding for Paul, much like when he came to understand
why nerve swellings occurred at particular points

in the body of leprosy sufferers. The leprosy bacilli preferred cooler temperatures to multiply, and they found such temperatures where the nerves ran close to the surface of the skin, such as above the elbow, at the ankles, knees, and wrists, and on the cheeks. To combat the growing population of leprosy bacilli at these locations, the body sent in armies of antibodies to attack and kill the bacilli. In the process, these antibodies caused swelling inside the sheath surrounding the nerve. The constricting effect of this swelling slowly cut off the supply of blood and killed the nerve. In the end, the leprosy bacilli did not cause the swelling. Rather, the swelling came as a result of the body's immune system trying to fight them off and in the process, killing a perfectly good nerve.

While Paul was grateful for the financial support his research received from the U.S. Department of Health, Education, and Welfare, the country's economy was worsening. More and more newspaper headlines were about some new government budget cut. With fewer than six thousand Hansen's disease patients in the United States, the argument was made that the research being done at Carville was not benefiting many Americans and was, in fact, benefiting more foreign sufferers of the disease. As a result, the U.S. government could no longer justify paying for such research. Paul sensed that it would not be long before he had to shut down some of his research projects.

Something wonderfully unexpected happened, however. One night while Paul was flipping through a medical journal, two words jumped out at him— *diabetic osteopathy*. Since osteopathy had to do with

bones, Paul wondered what diabetes, a disease affect-
ing the metabolizing of glucose in the body could
possibly have to do with bones? As he read the article, he was amazed to see pictures of X-rays of the
feet of diabetics that looked just like the X-rays of the
feet of leprosy patients. The two authors of the article
were based in Houston, Texas. When Paul contacted
them, they invited him to come to Texas to discuss
the topic with them.

The two doctors were intrigued as Paul showed
them X-rays of leprosy patients' feet that were almost
identical to the X-rays they had of diabetics' feet.
Paul realized that diabetes itself was not causing the
foot problems. Like leprosy, though from a different
cause, diabetes caused nerve damage. Without the
sensation of pain in their feet, diabetic patients did
not care for their feet properly. This was the same
problem that leprosy patients experienced with their
feet.

The doctors invited Paul to address the next meeting of the Southern Sugar Club, a group of diabetes
experts from the southern states who met regularly
to discuss the latest research on the disease. At the
meeting Paul presented his ideas about the similari-
ties in the causes of foot problems between leprosy
patients and diabetic patients.

Although his address to the Southern Sugar Club
was well received, Paul knew that many of those
present did not believe him. Many doctors told Paul
that he didn't understand. Even if he was right about
nerve damage causing the problem, diabetic flesh

would not heal, because of the lack of blood in the extremities. Paul felt like he was back at Vellore. It was the same old "bad flesh" argument he had heard so often regarding leprosy and which he knew was wrong. Already several diabetics had visited the foot clinic at Carville. Paul knew from thermographs of their feet that they still had enough blood flow in their extremities to heal from the ulcers on the soles of their feet.

Several months later, Paul received a call from Dr. John Davidson in Atlanta. Dr. Davidson explained that he had been at the Sugar Club meeting and had been skeptical of what Paul had said. Nonetheless, because of Paul's talk, he had employed a podiatrist at his diabetes clinic in Atlanta to examine the feet of patients when they came for a checkup. Much to his surprise he found that most of them had some kind of foot problem along the lines of what Paul had laid out in his talk. Also much to Dr. Davidson's surprise, in the previous year, 150 of his patients had received foot amputations, most of which he had not known about. Dr. Davidson explained that his patients came to him to have their insulin checked and to give blood and urine samples, but because they did not think he was interested in their feet, they said nothing about any foot problems they were having. When a patient did have a foot problem, he or she went to a foot specialist. Once the specialist realized that the patient was a diabetic, he or she would give up hope of the patient's foot healing and would order an amputation.

Armed with what Paul had told him at the Sugar Club and with a podiatrist now on staff at his clinic, Dr. Davidson was able to catch foot problems at an early stage before they had a chance to fester into much bigger problems. In fact, Dr. Davidson was so impressed with Paul's insights into the problem of diabetic feet that he asked Paul to prepare a chapter on the subject for a textbook he was writing on diabetes. He even sent his entire staff to Carville for special training from Paul and his team.

It wasn't long before word got out that the research being done by Paul at his foot clinic at Carville had more far-reaching applications than just to leprosy patients. Diabetes was a growing problem in the United States. Instead of slashing his research budget, the Department of Health, Education, and Welfare increased it.

Nothing could have pleased Paul more. Paul was profoundly grateful that his and Margaret's work at Carville could continue. As the years rolled by, one by one the children finished school and embarked upon their own careers. Christopher became a zoologist; Jean, a church worker in India and England; Mary, a nurse; Estelle, a preschool teacher; Pauline, a journalist; and Patricia, a doctor. All of them except Jean married and set up homes in the United States. Estelle married a young Hawaiian man who had come to Carville as a patient and had been successfully treated by Paul. Soon, Paul and Margaret had assumed the role of grandparents to seven grandchildren.

The couple continued to travel the world, advising, teaching, and inspiring another generation of leprosy caregivers. In fact, their speaking calendar filled up at least two years in advance.

Each year in October, Paul returned to Vellore to see how things were progressing, share new research and insights with doctors there, and teach in medical college. In 1974 he made two visits to Vellore, one in March with his daughter Jean and his regular trip in October. On both occasions his mother made the trip down from her home in the hill country to see him. She was now ninety-five years old and thin and frail. As always, she was feisty and totally committed to serving the poor people of the hill country. Each time Paul had visited his mother, he wondered whether it would be for the last time. October 1974 was the time. After his departure from Vellore, Evelyn had returned to her home in the mountains, but a month later she had returned to Vellore sick and more frail than ever. She stayed with Dr. Ernest Fritschi and his wife, Mano, and died at their house on December 18, 1974.

Paul was sorry to hear of his mother's death and wished he could have been there for the funeral. Now both his parents had died and been buried in India without his being there. Evelyn Brand's body was taken to Vazhavanthi in the Kolli Hills. The funeral service was held in the chapel that Paul's father had built years before, and her body was buried beside that of her husband. After forty-five years, Jesse and Evelyn Brand were once again side by side.

Although Paul had left the mission field to take up a secular position with the U.S. Public Health Service, his mission followed him. The Brands became active members in the Carville Protestant Chapel on the grounds of the leprosarium, where Paul often preached and held Bible studies. While Paul was content with that, his insights into Christianity from a medical viewpoint were about to be spread around the world. One day a young Christian writer named Philip Yancey came to hear Paul speak at the chapel and urged him to write a book. Paul confided that he had already written a manuscript but had never shown it to anyone. He went home to find it. He entrusted the manuscript to Philip, who took it and worked on it. Within months Dr. Paul Brand was on his way to becoming a best-selling author with the publication of his manuscript as the book *Fearfully and Wonderfully Made*.

When Paul officially retired from his job at Carville in 1986, he scarcely noticed a change of pace in his life. Margaret stayed at her post as head of ophthalmology for one more year. In September 1987, after twenty-one eventful years at Carville, it was time for the Brands to say good-bye to the many staff members and patients who had been their friends for over two decades. It was a time for tears but also a time for looking forward. Paul was now seventy-three years old, but he was not yet ready to just sit around all day.

Chapter 17

A Greater Loss

After leaving Carville, Paul and Margaret set up home in Seattle, Washington. They bought a small house on a hill overlooking Puget Sound. From their living room they could see the green and white Washington State ferries plying the water between Bainbridge Island and Seattle. They chose Seattle because Patricia and Christopher and their families lived nearby and because an international airport was within easy driving distance.

Paul and Margaret were no typical retired couple. One of the first things they did was hire a part-time secretary to help with their travel arrangements and answer the deluge of mail they received. The Brands continued to pour themselves into their leprosy work and Christian speaking engagements. The University of Washington honored Paul for his lifetime of medical achievements by naming him emeritus Professor of Orthopedics.

In May 1993, Paul and Margaret traveled to Montana to celebrate their fiftieth wedding anniversary. All their children were present, along with their twelve grandchildren. During the celebration the family presented Paul and Margaret with a handmade quilt made of photographs taken through the years. In the center was a photo of their wedding, Paul in his morning suit and Margaret in her wedding dress made from rationed fabric. The couple looked confident and trusting. They had no way of predicting that it would be three children and five years later before they would all be able to live in one house together as a family. Other photos on the quilt showed the children climbing trees in India and standing dutifully beside their aunts while on furlough in England. There was a photo of Granny Brand on horseback, her body hunched over but her spirit bright. There was also a photo of the staff and patients at Vellore—so many friends, so many good memories.

When Margaret saw the quilt, she burst into tears, and Paul struggled with his own composure. *How wonderful*, he thought, *to have lived such a full life, surrounded by so much love and so many amazing people.*

Indeed, Paul's long, full life was not yet over. Following the success of his 1980 book *Fearfully and Wonderfully Made*, Paul collaborated with Philip Yancey on a second book titled *In His Image*, published in

1984. Two years later Paul published a textbook, *Clinical Mechanics of the Hand,* which was used widely in medical schools and colleges. In 1993 he published two more books, *The Forever Feast,* and another collaboration with Philip Yancey titled *Pain: The Gift Nobody Wants.* The latter was an insightful book that sought to bring a new understanding of pain in human beings. Dr. C. Everett Koop, Surgeon General of the United States during the 1980s, wrote the foreword for the book. In his opening line he paid Paul the greatest of tributes: "Whenever I let my mind wander, and wonder who I would like to have been if I had not been born C. Everett Koop, the person who comes to mind frequently is Paul Brand."

Paul and Margaret continued traveling and teaching. Each year they visited Vellore to teach and visit with old friends and colleagues. They could no longer visit the facility at Carville, which in 1999 had closed down, though the research division was transferred to Louisiana State University in Baton Rouge. People still continued to contract Hansen's disease in the United States, but now the disease could be treated like any other disease at local clinics and hospitals. The days when leprosy patients had to be segregated from the general populace were over.

In August 2000, Paul and Margaret traveled to Vellore once again. This time it was to celebrate the one-hundred-year anniversary of the Christian Medical College and Hospital. Paul thought about his old friend Dr. Ida Scudder. What a visionary she had been when she arrived one hundred years earlier to establish the institution. How it had grown over time. Paul marveled at his own long association with the place. For fifty-four years his life had been closely intertwined with the hospital and medical college at Vellore. Even after he left India and his work at the institution, he had been back every year except one to teach at the medical college and consult with the doctors and surgeons.

In May 2003, Paul and Margaret celebrated their sixtieth wedding anniversary with a dinner party at the home of Patricia and her husband, Michael. One month later, on Margaret's eighty-fourth birthday, Paul fell down the stairs at their home in Seattle and banged his head. Margaret drove him to the hospital, where he underwent emergency surgery to relieve a blood clot on his brain. For two weeks following the surgery, Paul lapsed in and out of consciousness. Early on the morning of July 8, 2003, he died peacefully in the hospital, one week short of his eighty-ninth birthday.

A small, intimate graveside funeral service was held for Paul on beautiful Vashon Island in Puget Sound. The family wanted to say good-bye to their husband, father, and grandfather privately. They also understood that Dr. Paul Wilson Brand belonged to the world, and as many family members as possible attended memorial services that were held for Paul in Seattle, London, India, Africa, and South America.

Following his death, many obituaries were written for Paul, but none summed up his life better than

The Star, the newspaper Stanley Stein had started at Carville and was still being published from Baton Rouge.

> Dr. Brand's work lives through his dedication and encouragement to others. His skills, talents, spirit and humble humanity has made life worth living for all that knew him through service to his fellow man. A truly remarkable man, gifted and inspired beyond belief. He visualized a better and healthier world for all people and constantly worked toward this goal. . . . *No one knows who has suffered a greater loss; those of us who knew him, or those of you who did not.*

Brand, Margaret, and James L. Jost. *Vision for God: The Story of Dr. Margaret Brand.* Grand Rapids: Discovery House, 2006.

Brand, Paul W. *The Forever Feast: Letting God Satisfy Your Deepest Hunger.* Ann Arbor: Vine Books, 1993.

Brand, Paul W., and Philip Yancey. *Fearfully and Wonderfully Made.* Grand Rapids: Zondervan, 1980.

———. *In His Image.* Grand Rapids: Zondervan, 1984.

———. *Pain: The Gift Nobody Wants.* New York: HarperCollins, 1993.

Wilson, Dorothy Clarke. *Dr. Ida: The Story of Dr. Ida Scudder of Vellore.* London: Hodder and Stoughton, 1959.

———. *Granny Brand: Her Story.* Chappaqua, N.Y.: Christian Herald Books, 1976.

———. *Ten Fingers for God: The Life and Work of Dr. Paul Brand.* Paul Brand Publishing, 1989.

————————————————— *About the Authors*

Janet and Geoff Benge are a husband and wife writing team with more than twenty years of writing experience. Janet is a former elementary school teacher. Geoff holds a degree in history. Originally from New Zealand, the Benges spent ten years serving with Youth With A Mission. They have two daughters, Laura and Shannon, and an adopted son, Lito. They make their home in the Orlando, Florida, area.

Also from Janet and Geoff Benge...

More adventure-filled biographies for ages 10 to 100!

Christian Heroes: Then & Now

Gladys Aylward: The Adventure of a Lifetime • 978-1-57658-019-6
Nate Saint: On a Wing and a Prayer • 978-1-57658-017-2
Hudson Taylor: Deep in the Heart of China • 978-1-57658-016-5
Amy Carmichael: Rescuer of Precious Gems • 978-1-57658-018-9
Eric Liddell: Something Greater Than Gold • 978-1-57658-137-7
Corrie ten Boom: Keeper of the Angels' Den • 978-1-57658-136-0
William Carey: Obliged to Go • 978-1-57658-147-6
George Müller: Guardian of Bristol's Orphans • 978-1-57658-145-2
Jim Elliot: One Great Purpose • 978-1-57658-146-9
Mary Slessor: Forward into Calabar • 978-1-57658-148-3
David Livingstone: Africa's Trailblazer • 978-1-57658-153-7
Betty Greene: Wings to Serve • 978-1-57658-152-0
Adoniram Judson: Bound for Burma • 978-1-57658-161-2
Cameron Townsend: Good News in Every Language • 978-1-57658-164-3
Jonathan Goforth: An Open Door in China • 978-1-57658-174-2
Lottie Moon: Giving Her All for China • 978-1-57658-188-9
John Williams: Messenger of Peace • 978-1-57658-256-5
William Booth: Soup, Soap, and Salvation • 978-1-57658-258-9
Rowland Bingham: Into Africa's Interior • 978-1-57658-282-4
Ida Scudder: Healing Bodies, Touching Hearts • 978-1-57658-285-5
Wilfred Grenfell: Fisher of Men • 978-1-57658-292-3
Lillian Trasher: The Greatest Wonder in Egypt • 978-1-57658-305-0
Loren Cunningham: Into All the World • 978-1-57658-199-5
Florence Young: Mission Accomplished • 978-1-57658-313-5
Sundar Singh: Footprints Over the Mountains • 978-1-57658-318-0
C.T. Studd: No Retreat • 978-1-57658-288-6
Rachel Saint: A Star in the Jungle • 978-1-57658-337-1
Brother Andrew: God's Secret Agent • 978-1-57658-355-5
Clarence Jones: Mr. Radio • 978-1-57658-343-2
Count Zinzendorf: Firstfruit • 978-1-57658-262-6
John Wesley: The World His Parish • 978-1-57658-382-1
C. S. Lewis: Master Storyteller • 978-1-57658-385-2
David Bussau: Facing the World Head-on • 978-1-57658-415-6
Jacob DeShazer: Forgive Your Enemies • 978-1-57658-475-0
Isobel Kuhn: On the Roof of the World • 978-1-57658-497-2
Paul Brand: Helping Hands • 978-1-57658-536-8
D. L. Moody: Bringing Souls to Christ • On 978-1-57658-552-8

Another exciting series from Janet and Geoff Benge!

Heroes of History

Also available:

Unit Study Curriculum Guides

Turn a great reading experience into an even greater learning opportunity with a Unit Study Curriculum Guide. Available for select Christian Heroes: Then & Now and Heroes of History biographies.

Heroes for Young Readers

Written by Renee Taft Meloche • Illustrated by Bryan Pollard

Introduce younger children to the lives of these heroes with rhyming text and captivating color illustrations!

All of these series are available from YWAM Publishing
1-800-922-2143 / www.ywampublishing.com